FilmActresses

Volume 11

Mae West

Documentary study

Part 1

ISBN-13: 978-1503088214

ISBN-10: 1503088219

Dtp
and
graphic design

Iacob Adrian

Author statement

The actors and actresses are the the bricks .

The cast and crew are the plaster .

They stand on the foundation created by
producers and writers and directors .

All these people creates the great palace
of the art of film .

Iacob Adrian - 2013

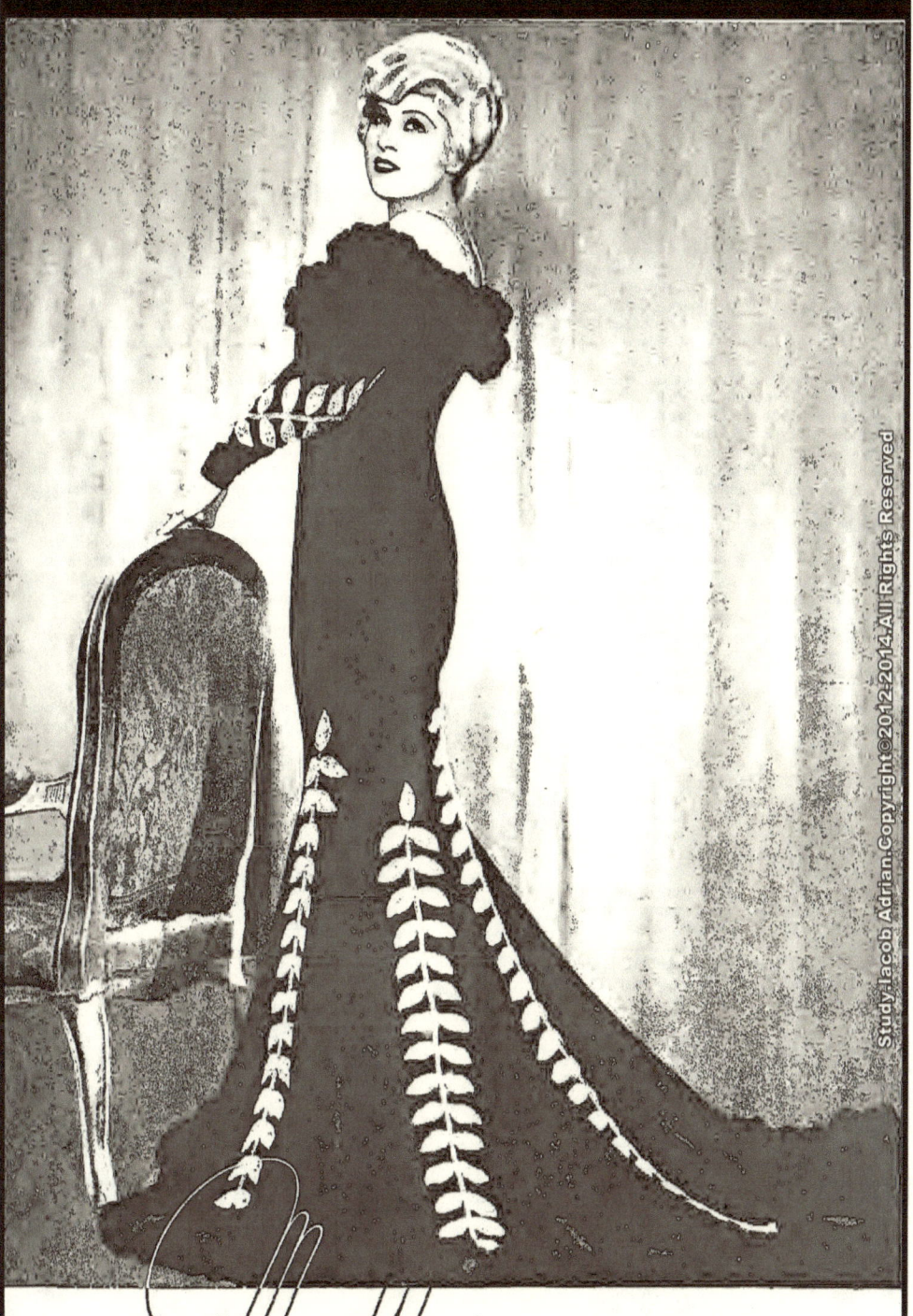

Mae West in "IT AIN'T NO SIN"
with Roger Pryor, John Mack Brown, Duke Ellington & Band...Directed by Leo McCarey
if it's a PARAMOUNT PICTURE...it's the best show in town!

Mae West's Personal

A fascinating revelation of the private life and character of the screen's most glamorous personality by the one who knows her best!

To Begin With, Libby Taylor isn't just an ordinary personal maid. She's an actress, and although Mae West pays Libby a maid's salary, she would be the first to tell you that Libby is an actress, and a good one! Years ago, before Mae West became MAE WEST, Libby worked with her on the stage. It is true that it was Mae West's company but Mae isn't the type to ever say "She worked *for* me"—it's always "*with* me."

Not so long ago, Libby needed a job and Mae needed a maid so they merged their wants and Libby went to work for Mae. Whether or not Libby is a good maid is hard to say. It isn't easy to imagine that the efficient Mae would even need a maid. Can you imagine Mae going hungry because the cook walked out? Neither can you imagine Mae going uncoiffed because the hair dresser failed to show up.

But, we weren't discussing the virtues of a maid. We were letting the maid discuss the virtues of a mistress, or "Muh Madam" as Libby fondly calls Mae West.

Mae West designed every bit of furniture in her bedroom. A color scheme of gold, green and a very delicate shade of pink is carried out in everything in the room, pillows, drapes, counterpane, upholstery—even the picture frames and toilet articles.

Although Mae is very tiny and dainty, she does not surround herself with dainty articles. She likes big things, "Something you can get your hands on," she explains. She has large perfume bottles, large cream jars, large powder boxes. Her daintiness running to materials and colors only.

Mae West always has her breakfast in bed, dressed in one of her many pretty negligees, with lacy pillows behind her back.

"An' is she a pitcha foh ya eye?" Don't ask Libby unless you really want to know, "Yes suh!"

● Libby explains that her greatest task in the morning is to keep Mae in a good mood, because if "Ah don't she kain't think up funny things to say, an' you *knows* she says funny things."

For breakfast Mae, according to Libby, has mostly fruits, a little toast, maybe a little egg or creamed chicken and coffee. She always has a good appetite and is not particular about how the tray looks provided there's plenty on it.

After breakfast, she wise-cracks all the way to the bathroom. She prefers a tub bath with plenty of hot water, scented soap and oodles of bath salts. And Libby thinks that's all right, "Ah likes 'em mah self 'couse they smells so good." Libby is worried about one thing, though, and that is how anyone can take a bath every morning and never say the same things twice, and yet say such smart and original things. We go Libby one better and wonder how anyone can keep up such

an original line of wise-cracks—bath or no bath!

If Mae is to spend the morning at home, she doesn't dress. She wears a negligee and we take Libby's word for it that it's "Moah comfoble like and relaxin'." And Libby's Madam never puts on makeup unless she is going out. "She doan need none to make huh pretty. She's jes natchurally beautiful, she is, like peaches with cream poared ovah 'em."

In this negligee, Mae does her home work of okaying bills, dictating letters or writing. At one time she wrote all her own material and only let the secretary copy it. That proved to be too slow and too hard work. Now she dictates everything—stories, novels and even the dialogue for her picture.

This gives her much more time and she also says that it makes it a little more natural just to "talk it off" than it does to sit down with a pencil and try to figure it out.

Don't we, who *think* we can write, wish we had a gift like that? It's a gift given only to a favored few!

● When I asked Libby what Mae does in her spare time, I received what I call a dirty look—and I deserved it. With a lifted eye-brow Libby replied, "Dat woman ain't got no spah time. If she ain't makin' a pitchah, den she's writin' huh next one, and if she ain't writin' a pitchah, she's writin' a story or a book or some dialogue or somethin'.' Sometimes she likes to go ridin' in huh cah, or to a show and everyone knows how she dotes on prizefights, but that ain't spah time—that's jes time! Ah couse, she goes to church, an' to see sick folks a lot an' tries to hep folks get work but she doan call that wastin' huh time."

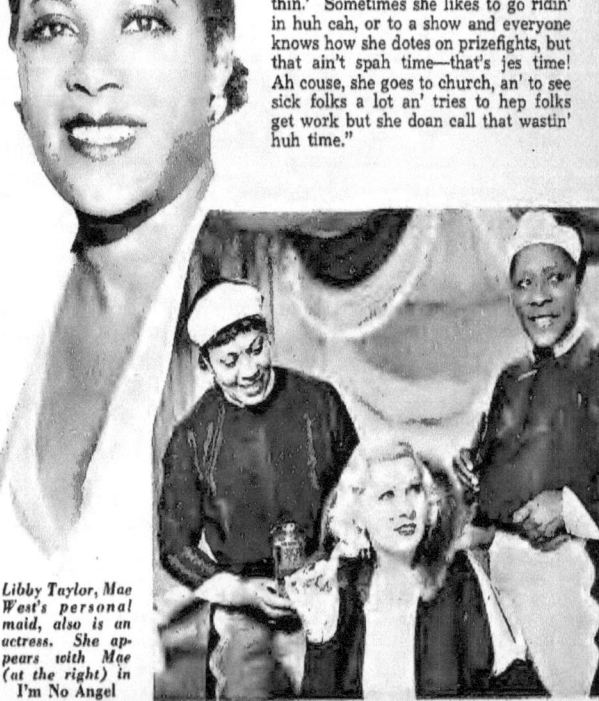

Libby Taylor, Mae West's personal maid, also is an actress. She appears with Mae (at the right) in I'm No Angel

Maid Tells ALL!

by
HARMONY HAYNES

Mae seldom goes shopping. As in the case of most stars, the shops are only too glad to send merchandise to her home on approval. But if she's buying a present for someone else she "goes right to the stoah and picks it out furst hand!"

Besides Libby and the secretary, Mae employs a chauffeur. She doesn't drive, she doesn't care to. She prefers to sit back among the cushions and think up stories or dialogue. She says she never thinks better than when the wheels are rolling under her—her mind sort of keeps pace with those revolving wheels, and the driver will tell you that he can always tell her moods by the way she asks him to drive—fast or slow.

The short distance between the car and Mae's dressing room requires from fifteen minutes to half an hour, not that Miss West is slow—you remember how she warbled, "I'm a fast moving gal what likes it slow"; but because everyone from the gateman to the president knows and adores her and isn't afraid to stop her long enough to say so. And their friendly greetings is Mae's morning tonic. Libby says "It peps huh up like nobody's business an' makes huh dimple all ovah!" Oh, Libby, Libby, you shouldn't have told us that!

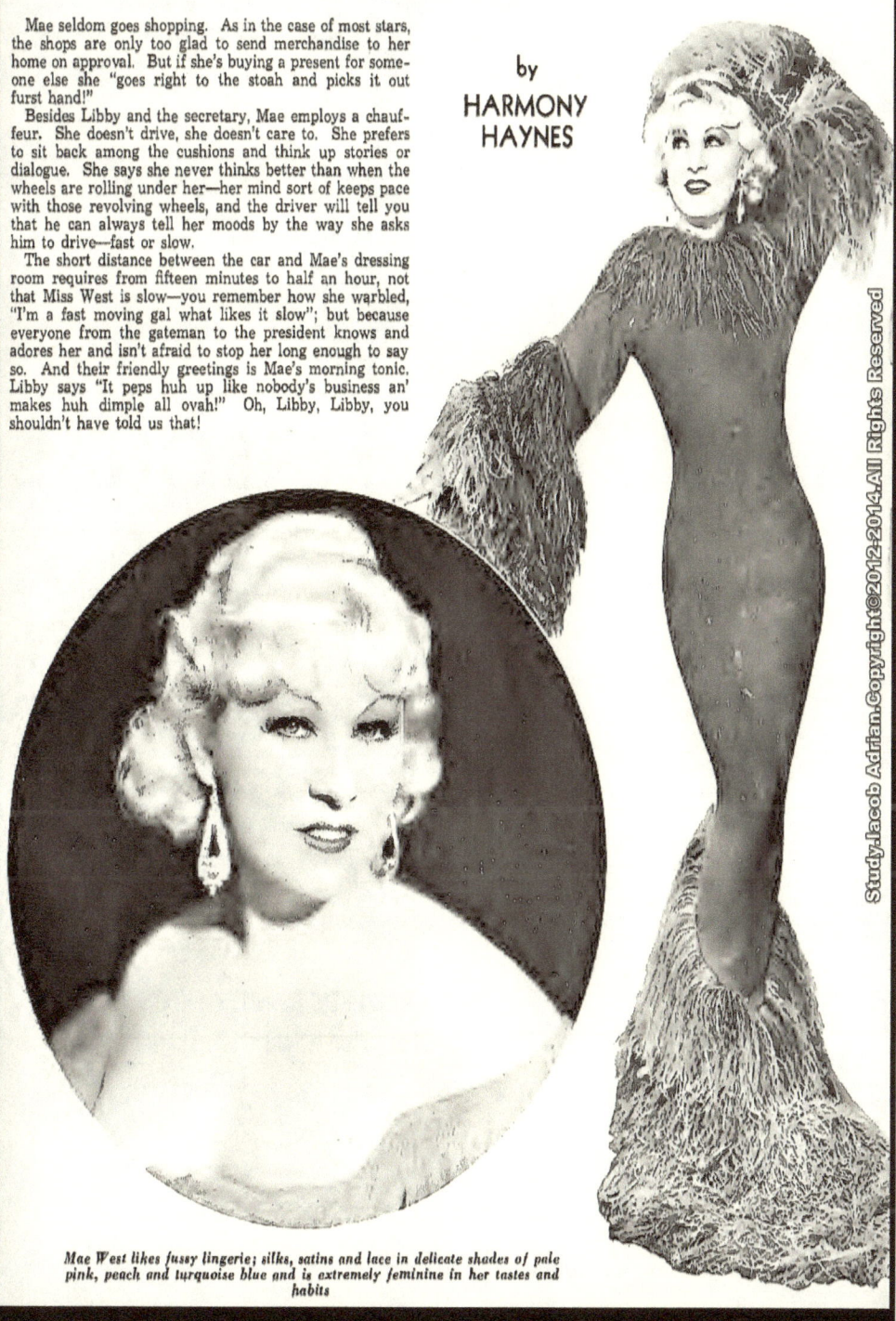

Mae West likes fussy lingerie; silks, satins and lace in delicate shades of pale pink, peach and turquoise blue and is extremely feminine in her tastes and habits

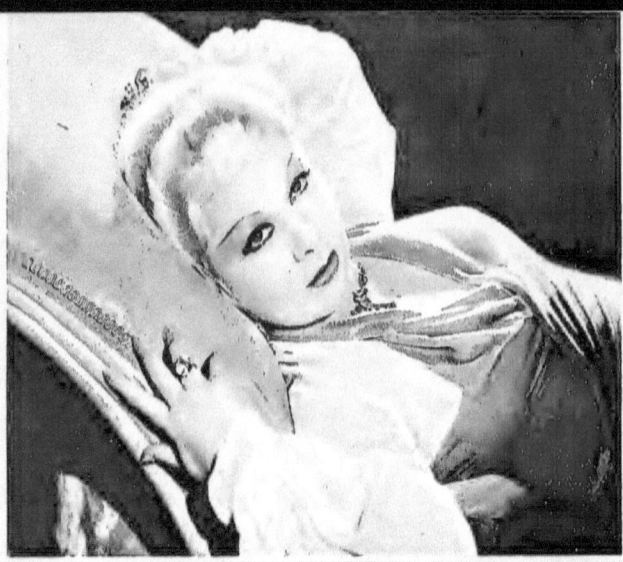

MAE WEST'S PERSONAL

"*I*T CAN be had. . . ." Mae West told me with one of those side-sweeping glances. "Call it beauty. Call it glamour. Go after it and you get it!" Hollywood has come to know it as the "Mae West MM-mmm" with plenty of accent on the first M. . . . Absolutely devastating, this "MM-mmm"—and twice as effective as "IT," "X" and all the rest.

You see, it's a sort of mesmerism. Complete feminine witchery. And don't think for a minute it's confined to a favored few.

"Eve had it," observed Mae. "And the whole female tribe inherited it—only some of them haven't learned that yet and others just let it dry up. You don't hear about *those* women, let me tell you. It's the Shebas and Helen of Troys—and the Diamond Lils—they talk about. Those girls knew they were Eve's daughters and no mistake! That is all that is necessary. You work up from there. Just get the old common sense in action and have a mirror handy. A full length one because these days it takes more than a face to launch a single ship, let alone a thousand. . . . But the face is as good a place to start with as any and that's where make-up comes in."

That is also where the "MM-mmm" begins!

● I've been cosmetician to the court of Russia and to the court of Hollywood for a total of more than half a century but I have never seen any woman with greater allure than Miss West. And no small part of it is due to her supreme skill in applying her everyday street make-up! After all, it's your "average" face that stamps you for what you are. Not the "dress-up" face over which you spend hours for special occasions. And Mae presents to the world at all times delicately heightened features with that "softened" look. Not a trace of powder or rouge is discernible. There is no emphatic dark line above the eyes.

That is a mistake frequently made by blondes especially—thinking their eyebrows must be as dark as their eyelashes. It gives them a hard, brittle look which men despise. But a woman with what we term "softness" in make-up instantly attracts. If she carries out that picture of ravishing femininity in voice and mannerisms as well as looks, you have this "MM-mmm" over which Movieland is raving.

"If you ask me," said Mae thoughtfully, "it isn't so much S. A. that counts with a girl as C. S.—that little old Common Sense I mentioned. It'll de-bunk this beauty business for her and tell her she's crazy if she thinks her come-hither ends with the eyes, nose and mouth. Or that powder three times lighter than her skin is going to make her fair as a day in

MAE WEST'S BEAUTY HINTS

*D*ON'T use heavy makeup. Not a trace of powder or rouge is discernible in Mae West's makeup which always has that "softened" look. There is no emphatic dark line above the eyes.

Blondes should not make their eyebrows as dark as their eyelashes. It gives them a hard, brittle look which men despise.

A bit of vaseline lightly applied over the eyeshadow helps to give makeup a soft look.

Never permit the lips to become dry or chapped.

In making up strive for a rosy glow that is gently accentuated over the cheekbones. Avoid any sudden spot of red.

In making up, smooth on a foundation cream, flesh colored, until it has entirely disappeared. Dip the fingers in cold water before blending the cream into the skin.

Pat rouge on very carefully with a puff, beginning at the temple and spreading over the cheeks. Blend it on the chin and then deepen it a trifle at the cheek bones. Shade the rouge by lightly patting the edges with the fingertips before patting on the powder.

Mae West's Personal Beauty Secrets

cheeks and chin and blended into the skin by fingers that have been dipped in cold water does the trick.

A<small>ND</small> N<small>OW</small> F<small>OR</small> that "warmth" which creates for blondes that impression of a tremendously vivid personality . . .

Take your rouge puff and your rouge box. With the puff pat on your rouge very, very carefully and very, very lightly, beginning at the temple and spreading over the cheeks. Then blend downward toward your chin. Now see that the color is deepened a trifle on the cheekbones. With your finger-tips blend the edges. Shade them so that your face has a glowing blush after you pat on your powder.

Mae West, you see, eschews hard, unnatural lines or color in her makeup for the same reasons she does smoking and drinking—they tend to coarsen.

"I don't believe in much massaging," she explained. "That wears down the tissue. For that reason I like a cleansing cream that melts as soon as it touches your skin so that you don't have to bother rubbing it in. But I'll tell you what I do . . . I rub off the first application of the cream. Then I pat on more cream and let it stay on while I'm taking my bath. The steam from the hot water opens the pores so the cream can do extra work. And when you finally rub it off, your face feels as clean as a chorus girl's conscience!"

But as we've said, the face is only the starting point of this magnetic "MM-mmm" business. Mae says clumsiness kills it more quickly than anything else. "And no woman needs to be clumsy! Did you ever think how lovely a girl looked sitting in a car—until she started to get out?

"Oh, I don't mean to start going in for studied poses, the Venus-at-the-sink sort of thing. Or for la-de-da gestures. But there are certain fundamental things that a girl can practice until they become a part of her—and they'll make her twice as easy to look at. That little matter of crossing the knees, for instance. They shouldn't be crossed at all. It's the legs which should be, and well above the knees, so that the top leg swings in the direction of the lower one and the calf isn't bulged out. The minute you let the hanging foot turn up your pose takes on an ugly line. Point the toes downward.

"I don't suppose there's any picture of a woman that remains with a man so as that of her pouring the morning coffee. If she wants to do right by herself she'll see that she does it gracefully. No using the elbows like flippers and letting them stick out at right angles to your body! And when you place those same elbows on the table in front of hubby, *be sure to keep them well together and close to the edge of the table.* This will keep your head and shoulders back and eliminate that disillusioning 'ho-hum' sprawl.

"And don't forget," she added, "that perfumes do stir the imagination. Try a little of your most delicate scent on the palm of your hand—then smooth hubby's forehead. It's a safe bet he won't go out that night!"

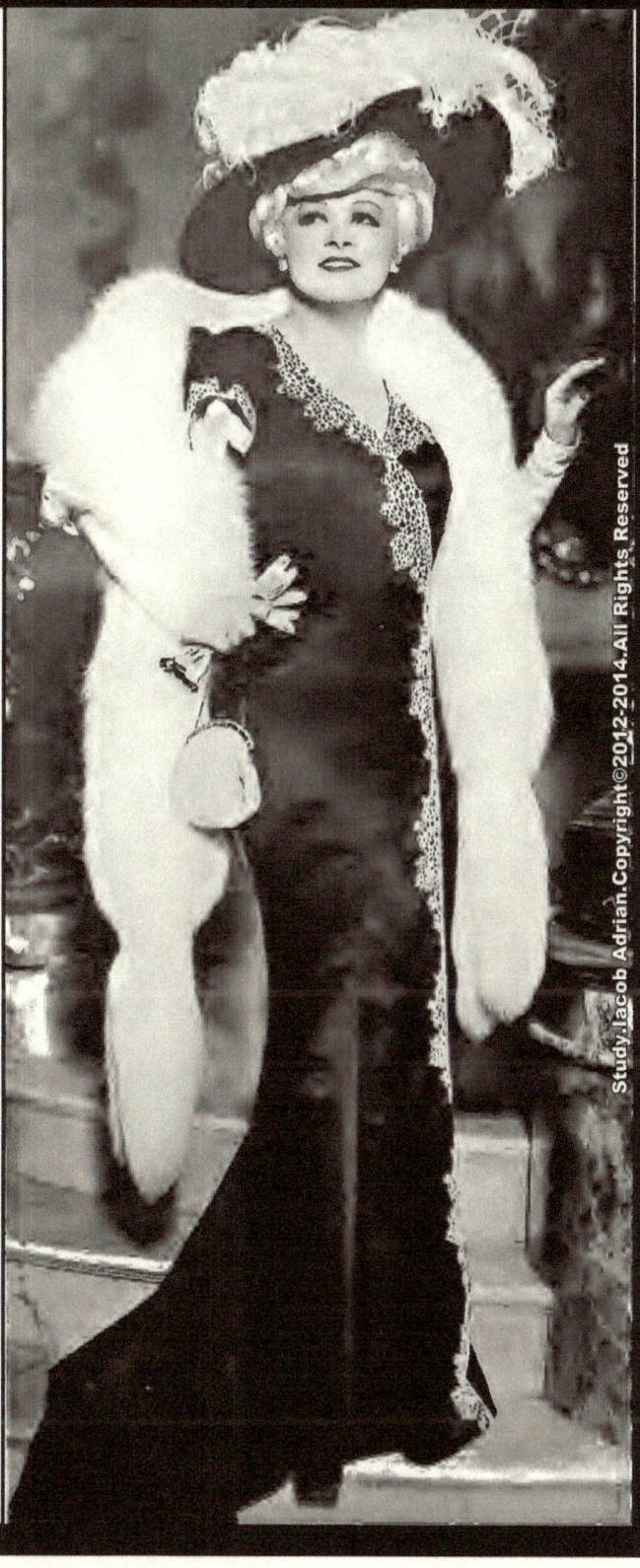

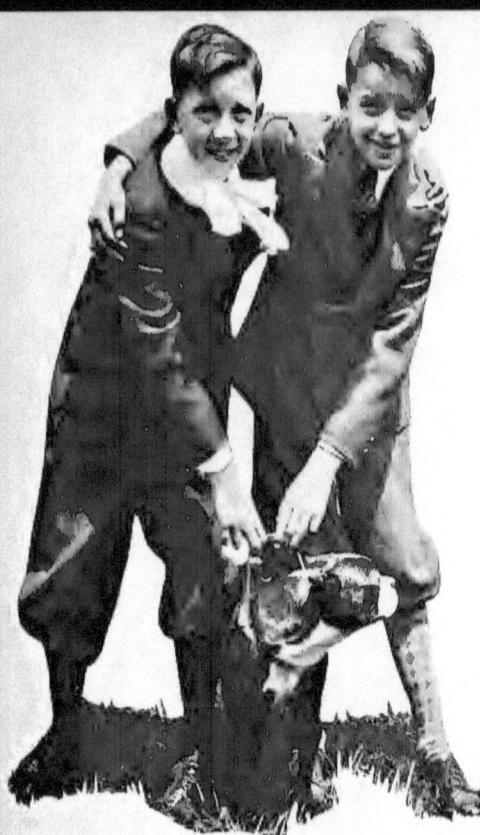

The Men in Mae West's Life!

Diamond Lil's true romance revealed in the most appealing story ever written about her!

by NED WILLIAMS

Jack Meuchner and Girard Thompson captured Mae West's heart and for ten years she has been their sweetheart!

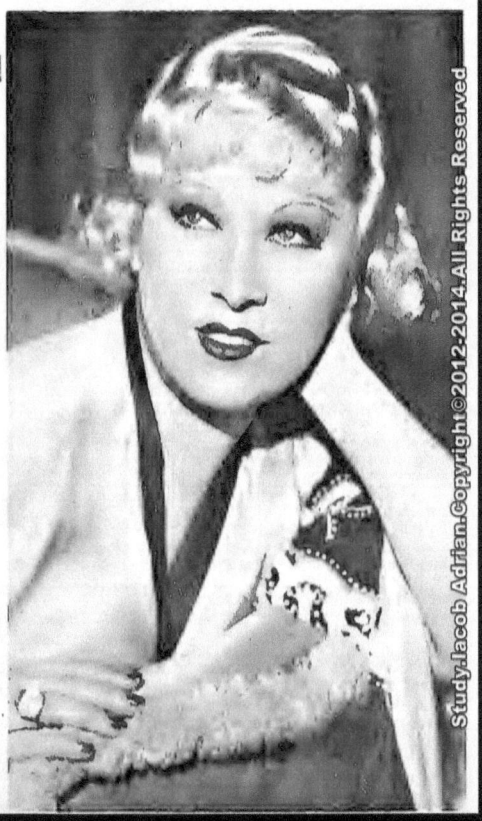

MAE WEST, THE GLAMOROUS, the alluring, whose fan mail of love letters from men all over the world reaches new heights every week, has promised her heart to two boys back home. They're only twelve now, but Mae has agreed to wait.

For nearly eleven years, Mae has watched the growth of two neighborhood children under her tutelage. She has trained them, taught them, counselled them. Their lives have been inextricably entwined with hers.

Near the corner of a wide street, miles past Brooklyn on Long Island, stands a freshly painted green and white house, so similar to a block of other houses on either side, that dark nights mean hopeless confusion to owners whose eyesight is poor or partially blurred.

This was Mae West's home until four years ago! Mae has moved, leaving Long Island for California and a new, richly furnished apartment in Hollywood. But her closest neighbors back home have remained, and her two boys are marking time until she comes east again.

Jack Meuchner and Girard Thompson, aged twelve, when interviewed, agreed on just two things: That they run their neighborhood together, and that Mae West is their sweetheart. In fact, she has been for ten years.

At Easter two huge baskets arrived at their two modest homes on Long Island. They were filled with all those delicacies which appeal most to young boys, but the only thing that thrilled Jack and Girard was a white card with Mae West's name engraved on it. It was further proof to them that Mae is keeping her promise.

The Men in Mae West's Life

THE COURTSHIP started when the boys were two years old. Mae was just beginning to startle vaudeville audiences into applause with her amazing new movements on the stage. Sex, as far as New York was concerned, had never really reared its head until Mae West perfected her art.

Mae was rapidly becoming a neighborhood celebrity. Those living nearest to her were awakening to the fact that there was a rising star of the stage in their midst. It was at this time that Mae became acquainted with Jack and Girard.

"I've never seen a girl who was so crazy about children," Jack's aunt, Mrs. Theodore Weigand, recalled. "But she ran true to form even then. She wanted what they called 'boy children.' Girls never did appeal to her."

The friendship blossomed in no time at all. Jack and Girard weren't sure about the sweetheart angle then, but they did know that if they toddled across the street and into Mae's house, they were sure of the warmest welcome of their lives. Before long, the only time they spent at home was eating and going to bed.

At Christmas, that first year, Mae decided the boys were old enough to learn the manly art of boxing. Her father, Jack West, then a professional fighter of some fame, agreed. So when the big morning arrived, Jack and Girard found huge boxing gloves under their trees, with a card of warning from Mae that the gloves were to be used.

It took Mae some time before she could say to herself that her two protégées were making any progress. They had difficulty at first in even standing up with boxing gloves on their hands, but by the next Christmas they could stretch out on their toes and swing at each other with real vehemence.

"It was Mae's ambition," Mrs. Weigand said, a faint smile of approbation on her lips, "to have the boys the champs of the neighborhood. I'll have to admit that she succeeded."

While Mae was working in vaudeville, with its attendant late hours, she found it hard to get enough sleep and still see her two boys every day. She finally found a solution—she had them come over in the morning while she was still in bed.

Jack and Girard would run over, their boxing gloves tucked under one arm, and race upstairs to Mae's bedroom. Bursting in on a tired and heavy-eyed Mae, they would clear the room until a small ring had been squared.

"Look, Mae!" Jack would shout. "I've got a new punch I wanna show you. Girard and I'll have a swell fight this morning."

"Okay, boys," Mae would reply, wide awake and eager to see the latest trick in fighting.

Wham! Jack would catch Girard off balance. In a minute Girard would retaliate. In another minute Mae would have to jump from bed and separate the two.

"They never could decide who was the better of the two," Mrs. Weigand said. "Mae couldn't, either. She would have them fight it off every so often, but it always ended in a draw."

SOMETIMES AFTER a fight, Mae decided that her two amateur boxers deserved a reward for their efforts. With a shout across the street to Jack's uncle, Mae would rush the boys downstairs to get the garage doors open. In a few minutes the three of them were outside, while the uncle fought to get the old model T Ford started.

Then for the ride! Each excursion they took was the thrill of a lifetime for all three of them. Out over Long Island, down to Brooklyn, a glimpse of roaring Manhattan; Mae at the wheel urging old Nellie on to greater speeds.

The boys soon grew old enough to have school interfere with the courtship. Winter mornings were no longer as carefree and happy for Mae. Jack and Girard had to sit in a room filled with students, counting the time until they could leave and hurry back to see Mae at lunch.

Summers were the same, however. Mae bought them cowboy suits. The neighbors objected a little at first to the bloodcurdling war-hoops that suddenly burst out behind garage doors, but Mae took the boys' side. As far as she was concerned, it was just another way for them to grow into strong and active young men.

Mae, at this time, was being showered under by floods of invitations for parties, dinners, dances. The neighbors watched with interest to see what effect popularity and adulation would have on Mae. Here is what one of her closest friends remembers about those days:

"No, Mae West was never the gay one she pretends to be on the stage and in the movies. It always seemed strange to me that such a vivacious and beautiful

—Bert Longworth

Aline MacMahon's constant companion when resting in her garden at home is this favorite spaniel. She is completing **A Woman in Her Thirties**

girl would prefer to stay home with her mother.

"In all the years I knew her, I can't remember a single wild party that Mae ever attended, and in this neighborhood it's pretty hard to do anything like that without having someone know about it."

"Sure she was popular," Jack said with a shrug of his already wide shoulders, "but she stayed home. Girard and me were too young to go out."

Then Mae wrote and produced *Sex*, the play that all Broadway still remembers and still talks about in awed tones. The first year of its run, nothing much was said against its being bad for public morals. Suddenly, public officials swooped down on an evening performance, closed the doors and arrested the performers.

Public indignation was at its highest. Mae West was painted as gaudy and publicity seeking. Those who knew her only through her acting were spreading stories about her. But her neighbors, those who knew her private life, stuck by her!

"I went with my baby one afternoon to see Mae," another neighbor recounted. "It was while *Sex* was running without interference from the city. When I saw her in her stage costume, my eyes nearly popped out of my head.

"Then Mae showed me how she had padded her shoulders and hips. When I told her she was no more like her stage part in real life than I was, Mae laughed and agreed with me."

Jack and Girard weren't quite certain just why the show was closed, but they did know that Mae had to serve ten days in jail. If they had known where to go, they would have been glad to take on the warden and free their idol.

THE SADDEST DAY in their young lives came at this time. Mae told them she was moving. Success was hers at last and Mae needed living quarters closer to town. No, she confided, she wasn't selling her house. Just renting it out to someone.

Although Mae was no longer just across the way, the two boys were not without her friendship. She made frequent trips back to the familiar old street to see them and give them advice.

Even the distance between New York and California failed to end the courtship. Mae came back to New York as soon as she could, and hurriedly took the long, tedious journey out through Long Island to call on them.

Mae appeared anxious when she visited her two boys. "What neighbor is having a hard time of it?" she asked them as soon as they had greeted her. "Who hasn't enough money to live on?" When they told her of a needy case or two, Mae took immediate steps to see that their suffering was relieved.

Right now Jack has a cousin who is just past the three-year-old mark. Mae has only seen him once or twice, so Jack and Girard don't consider him a real rival. There is another thing that worries them, though.

As yet Mae has not sent Theodore, junior, any boxing gloves. Is Mae weakening, they wonder? Has Hollywood finally won her over and reformed her with its softening influence?

The question will have to wait until next Christmas when Mae's gift box arrives, unless Mae comes to New York sooner than that. When she does, Jack has a new left to the jaw he'll use on her if he thinks she has changed any!

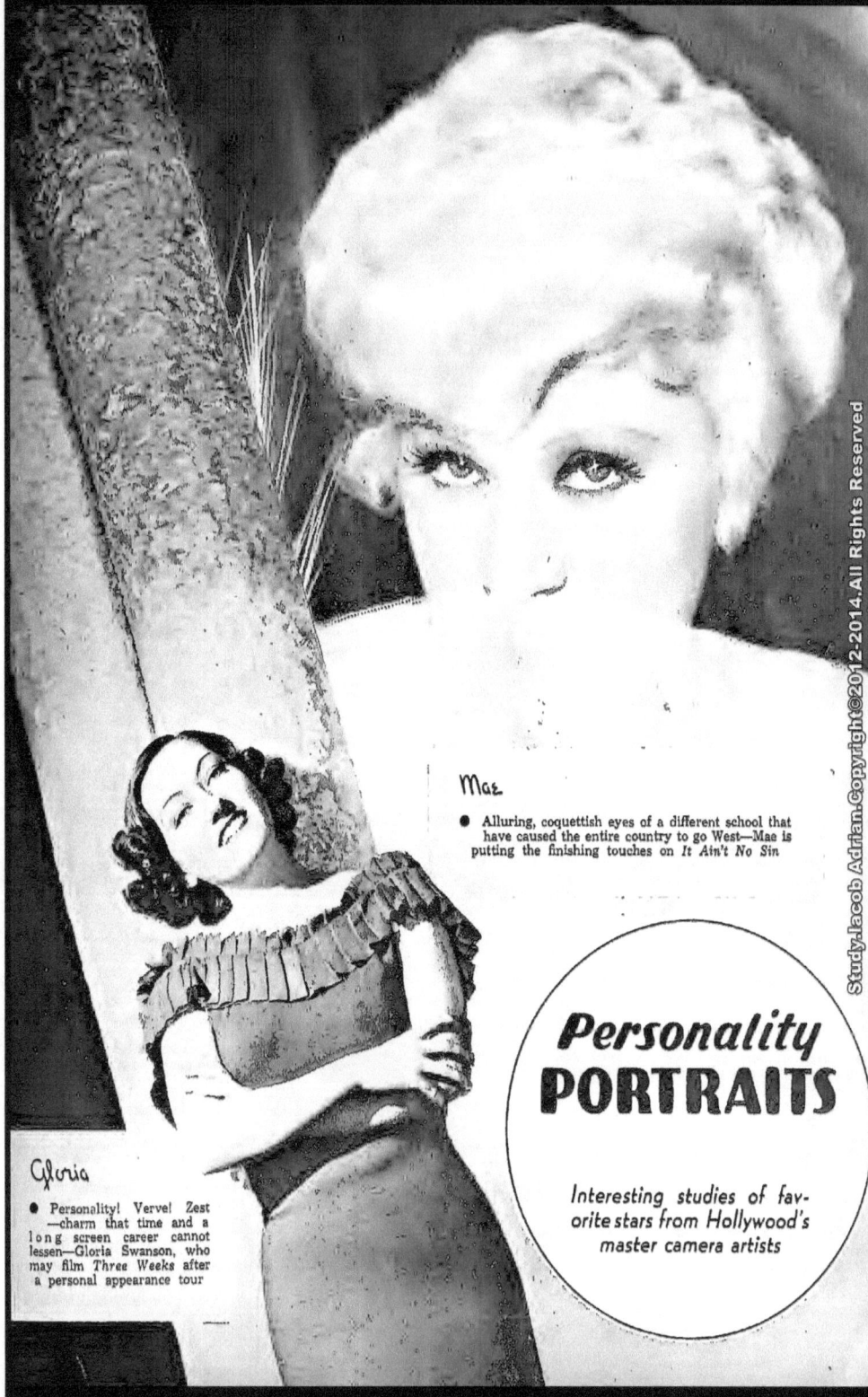

Mae

- Alluring, coquettish eyes of a different school that have caused the entire country to go West—Mae is putting the finishing touches on *It Ain't No Sin*

Gloria

- Personality! Verve! Zest—charm that time and a long screen career cannot lessen—Gloria Swanson, who may film *Three Weeks* after a personal appearance tour

Personality
PORTRAITS

Interesting studies of favorite stars from Hollywood's master camera artists

Pointed comment on movie events and affairs
by a noted film critic and writer

Harry Carr, one of Filmdom's most
popular and talented writers, offers his
sprightly comment here monthly

Anna Sten

NEVER HAS a girl hit Hollywood
who caused the producers so
much intense wear and tear as
Anna Sten, the lovely Russian girl.

They had to keep her in hiding for
a year while she learned English; now
they are simply frantic in their effort
to find a story for her. Even Vicki
Baum has thrown up her hands in de-
spair. Sam Goldwyn would pay almost anything imaginable; but there
just are no stories floating around
Hollywood.

Once, they thought they had an in-
spiration in the way of a story about
a circus rider who became a great
court lady during the reign of the
Emperor Maximilian in Mexico. To
their dismay, they l e a r n e d that
Mexico will permit no stories to be
shown that relate to the tragic Haps-
burg.

Katie Hepburn

I THINK that Katharine Hepburn is
making a mistake for which she will
be sorry. She has worn out the first
pert surprise she gave Hollywood in
veiling her own affairs from the public
eye. Katie is becoming snooty. She
has been one of the greatest hits in the
history of Hollywood . . . but . . .
but—

Spitfire was more spit than fire. I
think I shall send her a phonograph
record from an old opera called Havana
which had one song that might interest
her: Then Along Came Another Little
Girl.

The Big Old Bear

THERE IS AN actor in Hollywood,
Ivan Lebedeff, who is extraordi-
narily good at comparative physiog-
nomy — comparing men to animals.

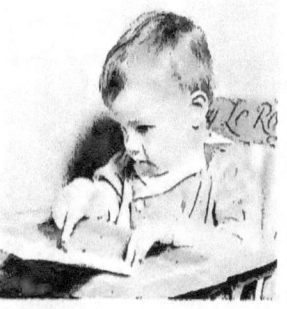

Baby LeRoy, a busy lad these days, does
a little pencil work on the script of The
Old-Fashioned Way, his latest picture

Some of his comparisons are not flat-
tering; but some are immense.

The reason that Wally Beery has
such an appeal is that all people in-
stinctively love bears; and Wally is
a bear . . . a shaggy, roaring, mis-
chievous old monster, who is likely
at the most unexpected moments to
turn over and bite his toes.

Valentino was a spir-
itual mixture of horse
and panther; Mary Pick-
ford was a pony, who
delighted t h e children;
Norma Shearer a thor-
oughbred race horse.

Lebedeff says that Doug
Fairbanks Sr. is a horse;
but it seems to me that
he is more like a big
courageous, frisking dog.

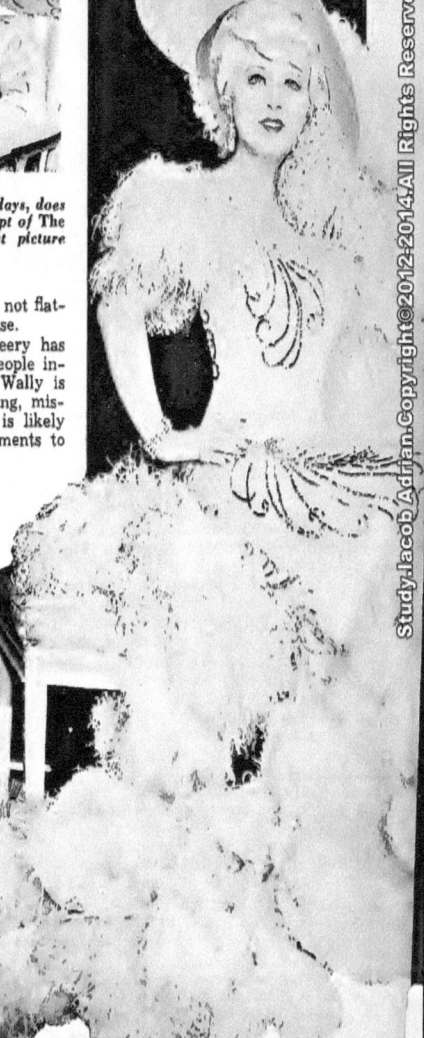

Mae West wears 100
ostrich plumes on this
elaborate costume for It
Ain't No Sin

by JERRY LANE

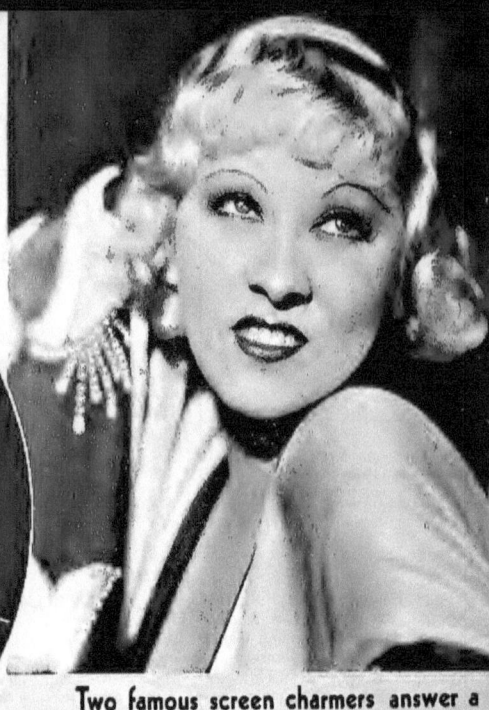

I'd fight to hold my man! — Mae West

Two famous screen charmers answer a

"Any women can get any man these days. But she's got to be good to keep him," says Mae West

"IF HE'S NOT WORTH fighting for, he's not worth having!" Mae West put plenty of punch behind that statement. The West eyes blazed with the light of battle. And when they blaze. . . !

"Listen, baby, 'it ain't no sin' to wage a good stiff war to keep your man. There were more than 200,000 divorces last year in this country. And if half of those wives hadn't been weak-kneed they wouldn't be wandering widows now! Any woman can get any man these days. But she's got to be good to keep him—better than her grandmother was by several hundred hot-cha degrees!

"You see," went on Mae, warming up to her subject as only she can, "every man seems always at least potentially in circulation. That's his nature. If you've got an interesting or attractive husband you can expect to face daily competition and comparison. There are plenty of sweet young things ready to get an unhappy man adrift. So—*anchor* him! Here's the way of it—

"If a girl finds she's losing hold on her man —and we're taking for granted he's the guy she can't possibly live without—she shouldn't waste time sympathizing with herself. Or wondering what's the matter with the man. Or trying to argue him into behaving himself.

"Just let her ask herself: *What's the matter with me?* Why doesn't he love me as much as he used to? What have I done? What *haven't* I done that he's giving me the chill?

"If the girl is frank, she might find that she has fallen

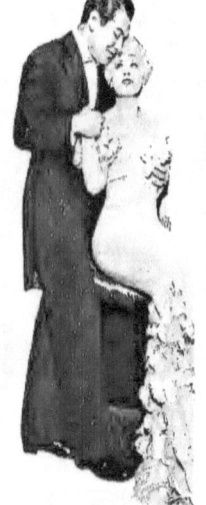

Mae West and John Mack Brown in a scene from St. Louis Woman in which she practices the wiles she recommends for real life

into the habit of treating the man like just another possession. Perhaps she is not making herself as attractive to him physically and mentally as she did when they lighted the torch. Maybe she's forgotten to be the playmate as well as the wife. *You can't be a spineless quitter if you want to hold your man!* You've got to understand his moods and know how to handle him when those moods are upon him. When he wants affection give it to him. When he doesn't, don't try to force it on the poor fellow. Anticipate his likes and dislikes so that you are continually captivating him with pleasant surprises. Men love surprises. They're a good deal like kids. When he expects a scolding, give him smiles.

"In short, try to make yourself so completely desirable, so utterly necessary to his well-being and fit into his life so charmingly that he'd rather go out and cut his throat than look at another girl.

"That all sounds like a pretty tough job, doesn't it? It is. But that is what fighting to hold your man consists of."

● Of course Mae wants it distinctly understood that she doesn't mean for a woman to bury her own personality and be entirely overshadowed by the man. On the contrary, the more she keeps herself an *individual*, the more he's apt to respect her.

This is one of the favorite West subjects. She has studied it out in many a drama of the sexes. A large

"If he's not worth fighting for he's not worth having!"—Mae West

"If you have to struggle to hold a man's affection he isn't worth the effort!"—Jean Harlow

No man is worth fighting for! —Jean Harlow

question of vital interest to every girl

"You're defeating your own purpose when you think you have to fight to hold your man," says Jean Harlow, who is shown here with Franchot Tone

"IF YOU HAVE to struggle to hold a man's affection he isn't worth the effort!" That is how Jean Harlow summarizes it. Jean, who typifies all the freedom and independence of the new era. Who is as modern as tomorrow—and just as unpredictable.

Jean, at twenty-two, has been married three times. Mae West, at thirty-two, has never been married. Both are the kind of women men can't forget. Sensational screen sirens. Glamour girls who know all the answers—but they differ on this one. Listen to what Jean says:

"You're defeating your own end when you so much as think, *I have to fight to hold this man.* You're placing a terrific handicap on your romance. Because you are implying *doubt.* Doubt in your husband, doubt in yourself. No love can live under such conditions. If you enter into marriage with the idea that it's going to be an endurance contest and all other women are your opponents—well, you might as well say 'Good morning, judge!' right then and there.

"I know a girl who had that thought. Just before the wedding bells chimed a wiseacre aunt whispered to her, 'Now, Ann, my dear, *remember* Bill is your particular property. Don't let him out of your grasp for a minute.' And Ann didn't. If Bill came home tired and kissed her a little abstractedly it was a sure sign to her way of thinking that she was slipping in her looks. So she'd go out and get a new dress and an expensive facial.

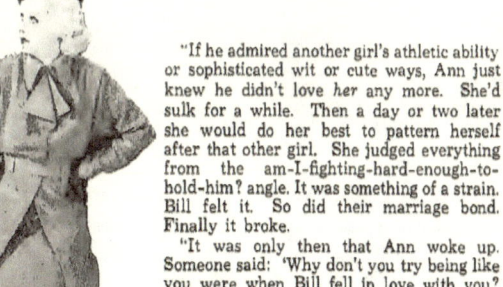

"I know I fight to hold my men on the screen," Jean Harlow says, "but you're placing too great a handicap on romance when you do this in real life"

"If he admired another girl's athletic ability or sophisticated wit or cute ways, Ann just knew he didn't love *her* any more. She'd sulk for a while. Then a day or two later she would do her best to pattern herself after that other girl. She judged everything from the am-I-fighting-hard-enough-to-hold-him? angle. It was something of a strain. Bill felt it. So did their marriage bond. Finally it broke.

"It was only then that Ann woke up. Someone said: 'Why don't you try being like you were when Bill fell in love with you? Don't work so hard at trying to fascinate him.' It was the soundest advice in the world. They're remarried now. And happy.

● "Why should a woman be different after marriage anyway? Why shouldn't she go right on being a man's sweetheart and treating him like she did when they were engaged? There's no need to take that terribly possessive air with him. He's a free individual. So are you. It's the worst mistake a woman can make to attempt to change herself into something she's not—or to attempt transforming her husband!

"A man falls in love with you because you have certain qualities. Don't alter them after the last of the rice has been thrown. Accentuate them. Do your utmost to make the type you are outstanding. To be definitely, clearly *yourself.* Your best self. Then if you fail, you can't have any regrets." Jean shrugged. There

I'd Fight to Hold My Man

portion of the unhappiness in the world, she claims, is due to lack of the proper sort of spunk on a woman's part—and lack of using her head with her heart.

"Now comes the question of the Other Woman." Mae looked thoughtful. "What should a girl do when it has reached the point where her man is resting another head on his shoulder or even thinking about it?

"If the prescription I've already mentioned is taken in time I don't believe there can be any Other Woman. But if the O. W. has muscled in on your exclusive territory before this, something must be done at once. That is, if you still think your man is worth scrapping for.

"Should you set yourself to give said Other Woman a terrific shellacking at the first opportunity? I wouldn't. If you beat her up—with words or fists—you'd only make your boy friend sympathize with her. What to do then? Step out yourself and make your man jealous? That doesn't work out well except in one case in a thousand. It's sure to stir up a lot of argument and common ordinary brawling between you and your man, and when it boils down to that you might as well put on your hat and coat and consider it all washed up.

"I'd say the best way out of the O. W. problem is to be so attractive yourself that no other woman will stand a chance. I don't just mean by 'attractive' that a woman has to be beautiful or even pretty. Attractiveness combines one's manners; one's ability to be pleasant and 'likeable.' In brief, it is the front that you show to the world backed up by what you feel inside of you—the total effect of your whole personality that makes you engaging or not.

"I CAN'T GIVE any capsule formula for holding a husband. I don't believe there is any. But if you are in fear of losing your man and you want to hold the brute, fill his evenings. Fill his thoughts. But don't make it obvious that you're after his admiration. No fight is going to produce results unless you're able to create for him the illusion at least that you are indispensable to his life. Fight *subtly*. Gaiety and humor mixed with a dash of mystery are the finest weapons.

"And by mystery I'm not referring to any cold aloofness," Mae hastened to explain. "Keeping a man guessing is usually a good piece of business for a single girl but it usually gets a wife into trouble. A woman who makes her husband worry and wonder too much is apt to be pretty irritating around a home. Very likely he'll turn to someone else who doesn't afford so much guess-work! No, by mystery I mean simply to exercise a certain amount of reserve in her relations to others and create an atmosphere of self-containment. It makes a man think about her. It makes him want to know why she is that way and how she got that way! He will want to break down that reserve and disturb that self-assurance. Frankly, no woman should be as easily readable as an open book. She should control her emotion just enough to provoke a man's curiosity.

"Fight? You bet you should! It's a wrong idea of sportsmanship to bolt the minute the third angle of a triangle shows her head. Boys and girls these days know the physical facts. But they're ignorant of the things that really matter. That a man's and woman's love is something to be held and sacrificed for—yes, and *fought for*."

◆

No Man Is Worth Fighting For

was something a little pitiful about that shrug.

No girl ever wanted more to make a success of her marriage than Jean did. Now at the end of eight months she finds her romance with Hal Rosson, that started out so gaily with an elopement at dawn to Yuma, ended . . . in divorce. She's facing a high wave of misunderstanding, sharp criticism, even rebukes for something I happen to know was as unescapable as Fate. And she's facing it with characteristic courage.

No, it isn't from any lack of stamina that Jean Harlow says, don't *struggle to keep your man.*

"Oh, I know I do it on the screen. I literally pull hair and strike and scratch for him!" she smiled. "Remember in *Red Dust?* And I even did a picture with the title, *Hold Your Man.* But in everyday living it's another matter.

"It's the *man* who wants to feel he's holding his woman against the world.

You do it and the first thing you know you'll be cajoling and mothering him and there's nothing a man hates more.

"Jealousy is only a form of distrust, a thing that kills love. It's *fear*—and that's what makes you want to fight. Throw away the fear of losing your husband. Let me tell you, the greatest romance in the world can't stand nagging! The most terrible thing a woman can do is to get her feelings hurt and pout. And that's the one way to get rid of the person you adore!

"It's a wise wife who can enter into the spirit of playtime with her man and not be too matter-of-fact; who knows how to offer him something when he comes home—varied interests, charm, a real smile of the just-for-you variety.

"To her, marriage won't mean a continual conflict for the love of a man. It will mean the security and happiness that every woman wants."

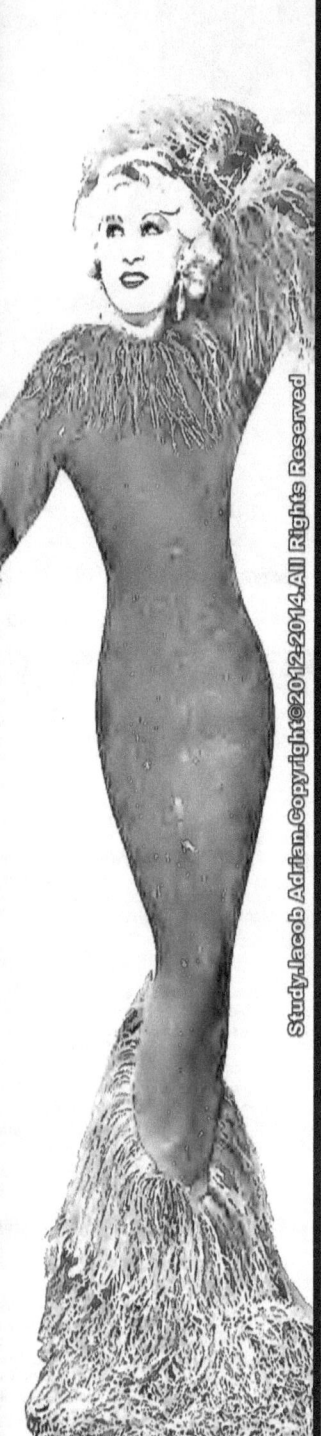

Mae West Should Get Married!

Read this daring story by a famous Hollywood writer in September

SCREEN BOOK

Other remarkable features in this issue: Margaret Sullavan's Mystery Husband Talks, The Mystery Man in Marlene Dietrich's Past, and outstanding stories about Alice Faye, Joan and Constance Bennett and Katherine DeMille

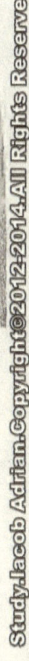

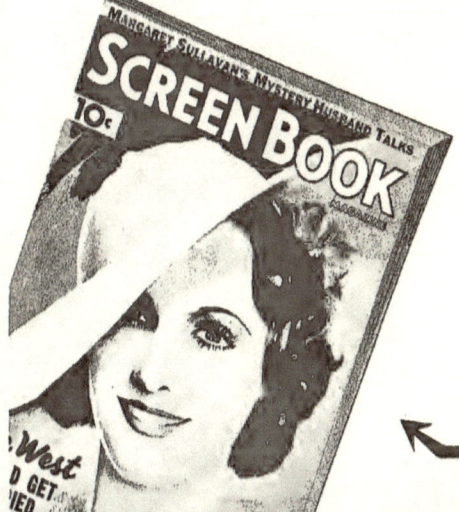

SCOOP!

Don't miss *The Tragic Story Behind Dorothy Dell's Death!*

FREE!

Secure valuable personal beauty advice from a Hollywood expert free of charge through SCREEN BOOK

LOOK FOR THIS COVER

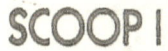

ON ALL NEWSSTANDS

• Coming events cast their shadows before

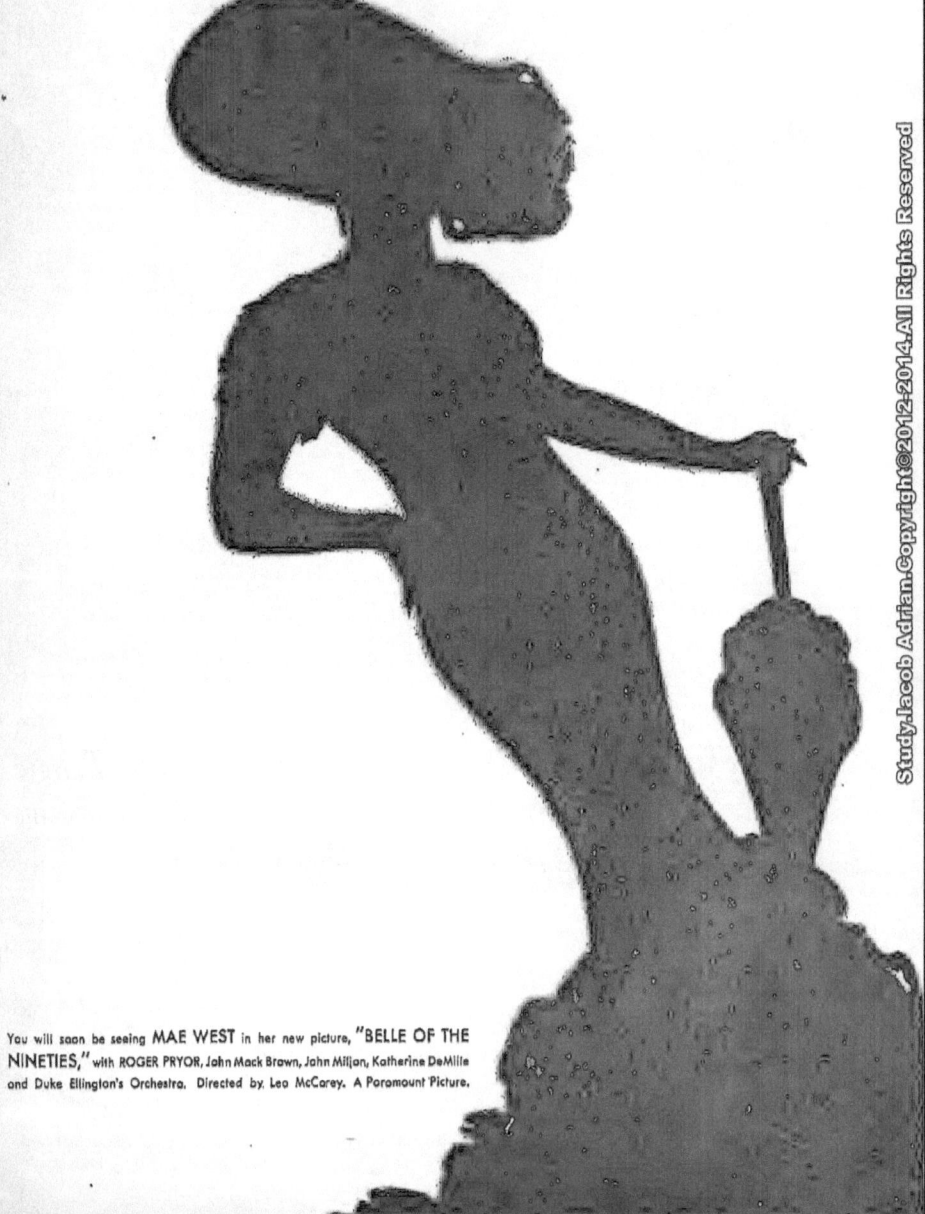

You will soon be seeing MAE WEST in her new picture, "BELLE OF THE NINETIES," with ROGER PRYOR, John Mack Brown, John Miljan, Katherine DeMille and Duke Ellington's Orchestra. Directed by Leo McCarey. A Paramount Picture.

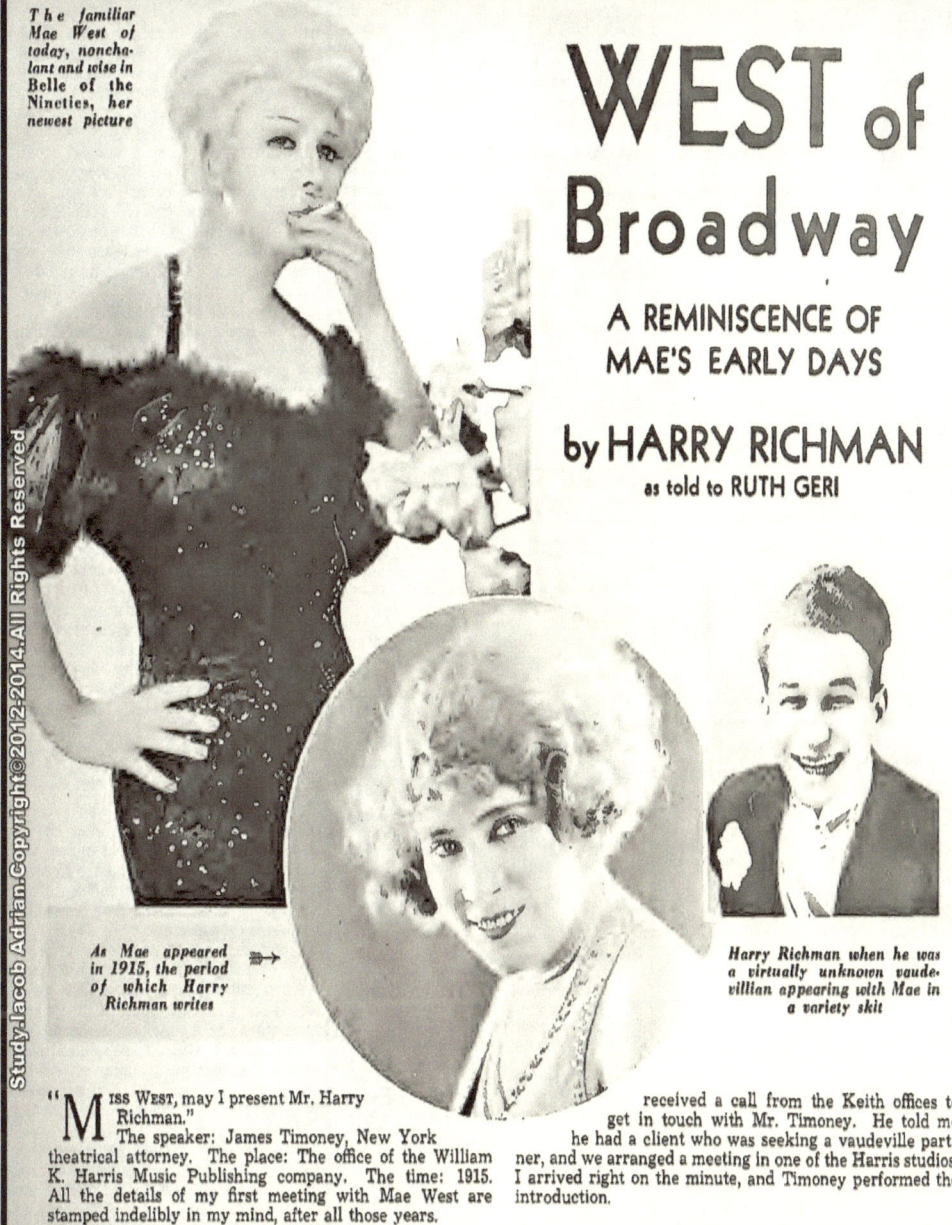

The familiar Mae West of today, nonchalant and wise in Belle of the Nineties, her newest picture

WEST of Broadway

A REMINISCENCE OF MAE'S EARLY DAYS

by HARRY RICHMAN
as told to RUTH GERI

As Mae appeared in 1915, the period of which Harry Richman writes ➡

Harry Richman when he was a virtually unknown vaudevillian appearing with Mae in a variety skit

"MISS WEST, may I present Mr. Harry Richman."

The speaker: James Timoney, New York theatrical attorney. The place: The office of the William K. Harris Music Publishing company. The time: 1915. All the details of my first meeting with Mae West are stamped indelibly in my mind, after all those years.

I had just returned from the Panama-Pacific exposition in San Francisco where, as a member of the Jewel City Trio, I had been appearing in fourteen shows a day. Take it from me, there are very few things you can do fourteen times a day without getting pretty tired of it all, and when I returned to New York, for once in my life I did not mind being out of work. Sleep seemed a lot more important than eating regularly. Before long, though, I began to think that perhaps eating fourteen times a day was something I wouldn't get tired of.

You can understand, then, why I wasted no time when I received a call from the Keith offices to get in touch with Mr. Timoney. He told me he had a client who was seeking a vaudeville partner, and we arranged a meeting in one of the Harris studios. I arrived right on the minute, and Timoney performed the introduction.

● It is hard to believe how like the Mae West of today the Mae West of 1915 appeared when I met her then. The same curves, bustles, curly blond hair, floppy picture hat and all. To see Miss West today one who knew her then might imagine that here was a present-day-female Rip Van Winkle, fresh from a twenty-year nap.

Her acknowledgment of Timoney's introduction was typical, and I must admit left me slightly ill at ease. She did not speak; did not even smile. Instead, her eyes swept me from head to foot, a long, appraising stare. I felt an

Please turn to page sixty-three

A revealing portrait by Mae's one-time piano player, now a noted stage star

Study Jacob Adrian.Copyright©2012-2014.All Rights Reserved

West of Broadway

attack of fidgets coming on. Then she spoke.

"Are you versatile?" she demanded in a low, crooning monotone, with a trace of what seemed to be skepticism in her intonation.

By this time my case of fidgets had passed the incipient stage. I felt like a schoolboy in the principal's office. But I did want that job! I replied with all the *savoir faire* (I didn't call it that at the time) that I could summon.

"That all depends on what you call versatile."

"Well, I need a piano player good enough to do specialty numbers while I change my clothes, and keep the suckers on the jump," she explained. "You've gotta be able to put over a song. You've gotta be a swell actor—able to feed lines and take 'em. You've gotta look like a million bucks on the stage, even on an empty stomach, and you've gotta be able to wear clothes.

"But above all," she concluded, "you've gotta have a certain something."

Listening To Miss West I concluded that her requirements called for a combination of Barrymore, Mansfield and Booth, combining the best features of each. But I did want that job! It struck me forcibly that Miss West might not be a particularly indulgent employer, but at the same time it occurred to me that my landlady was not a particularly indulgent landlady. So I summoned all my optimism to reply.

"As far as everything except the 'certain something' goes, Miss West, I'm pretty sure I can fill the bill," I boasted. "And as for the 'certain something,' you'll have to judge that for yourself."

Miss West, typically, wanted to be shown. She asked me to play the piano. I did, and waited hopefully for her comment.

"M-m-m-m-m-m-mmmm," was all that came. She trilled it. You know how I mean. You've heard her. I hadn't—until then. She asked me to sing.

"M-m-m-m-m-m-mmmm," once more. Then a long silence. My fidgets returned.

"I'll have the script tomorrow and you can run through your lines," she said at length with a gesture of dismissal. The next day I returned, ran through the script and was hired. Two minutes later came our first difficulty. Miss West wanted the act called *Mae West & Co.* while I held out for *Mae West & Harry Richman.* I pointed out that, after all, I had been a featured act in vaudeville, and finally won Miss West over. That little difference settled in my mind that Mae West was a square shooter and a sportsman; always willing to give the other fellow a break—even if she did make him fight for it.

We agreed on $500 for the act; $200 for me and the rest for Miss West. At the tryout it was a sensational success.

But how the manager howled! The act was raw, he complained. It was suggestive! He wouldn't stand for it in *his* house. Remember, this was 1915, and although the routine of *The Gladiator* was little different from Miss West's performances in *Diamond Lil, She Done Him Wrong* and her other subsequent brilliant successes, the inhibitions of 1915 and of the '30's were widely divergent. Par-

ticularly did the manager object to the shimmy with which Miss West accompanied her rendition of *Frankie and Johnny,* although the audiences howled gleeful appreciation. From each place we played a bitter complaint went to the Keith offices.

Finally Edward F. Albee, the Keith general manager, called us in and told us of the unfavorable comment our act was provoking. Miss West became highly indignant. She denied that there was the slightest basis for the complaints. The managers were evil minded, she told Mr. Albee, and to prove it she offered to do the act and let him be the judge himself.

Early the next morning we went to an empty theater—Mr. Albee, Miss West and myself. I was so nervous I could scarcely speak, for I knew Mr. Albee would throw up his hands in holy horror when he saw the act. But before we began, Miss West winked at me reassuringly and told me just to go ahead with my routine as usual. Then she put on one of the most remarkable performances I have ever seen.

Using the same lines, but altering a gesture here, eliminating another there, she made the act seem lily white. No one could conceivably have objected to any part of it. When she sang *Frankie and Johnny* and came to the line "If you don't like my peaches, why do you shake my tree," instead of the sly wiggle, she raised her arm like an operatic prima donna and her face assumed a perfectly angelic expression. The listener might have supposed she was singing a paen to the beauties and joys of Mother Nature.

Mr. Albee was sold. He expressed indignation at the complaining managers and assured us that henceforth he would refuse to listen to such tommyrot. The next day we were engaged at Proctor's Fifth Avenue with an audience composed for the most part of travelling men. Miss West put in everything she had omitted for Mr. Albee and added a few extra bits for good measure. The audience was in an uproar. We stopped the show. Then the manager stopped us. He insisted we tone the whole thing down. He said he just wouldn't have it.

"Now just a minute. Just a minute," Miss West interrupted. "Neither you nor I have any right to change this act. But if Mr. Albee wants it changed, of course that's different. Then I'll change it. Why don't you call him?"

The manager fell for it. He telephoned Mr. Albee. Before he could finish what he had to say, Mr. Albee interrupted him. "I don't want to listen to such silly talk as that," he roared. "I've seen that act, and it's perfectly all right. It stays the way it is, understand!" And the Keith headman angrily hung up.

Free From Such managerial interference, the act was a tremendous success. We stopped the show everywhere we played, but the trouble was that we didn't play many places. Miss West insisted on $500, and she wouldn't take $499, either. It was $500 or nothing, with the result that most of the time, it was nothing. During the fifteen months we were together we played a total of five weeks and my share for the fifteen months was a thousand dollars—a little more than $16 a week. I could make more than that selling dresses.

Miss West's consuming passion was to earn more than $500 a week. She felt

that she would then be a success. Time and again she refused flatly to compromise on price. Often we would walk out of a booking agent's office after she had haughtily turned down $400 for a week and in the corridor, she would whisper, "Say, Harry, lend me a coupla bucks, will you?" One time, the telephone in her apartment in Jersey City was disconnected because the bill hadn't been paid. I learned of a chance for a week's engagement and tried to reach her. No luck. I called Timoney, and he couldn't locate her either. By the time I finally got hold of her it was too late.

I was considering leaving her when she wrote a play. She felt sure that if we put it on it would mean fame and fortune for all of us. So Timoney and I "angeled" the show, if you could imagine two people as broke as we were "angeling" anything of greater magnitude than a cup of coffee. We begged and borrowed scenery and costumes. We cajoled electricians and stage hands. We talked actors and actresses into working on "spec." I was so nervous during those frenzied preparations and that hectic opening that to this day I can't for the life of me remember the name of that play. But I do remember that when we opened in Greenwich Village the show laid an egg that any ostrich would be proud to crow about.

I surveyed the wreckage and recalled the solemn promises I had made to obtain credit. I visualized my irate landlady; noted my decreasing waist-line.

"Mae," I said, "I admire you greatly. Your act is a wow. Your show should have been a hit and I cannot understand why it wasn't. But I must eat more regularly. This life is beginning to tell on me." We parted the best of friends and have remained so to this day.

I landed a short engagement with the Dolly sisters which ended when they went to Europe. I found myself "resting," as they call it in front of the Palace, once again. So for the next eight months I made a comfortable, if unexciting living selling dresses, and I might have been doing that still had not a good friend engaged me for a featured act at the Orpheum.

Miss West, brave, undaunted, her spirit unbroken despite all her reverses, carried on. She always said that someday she would hit; someday the public would appreciate her.

You know how her courage has been rewarded.

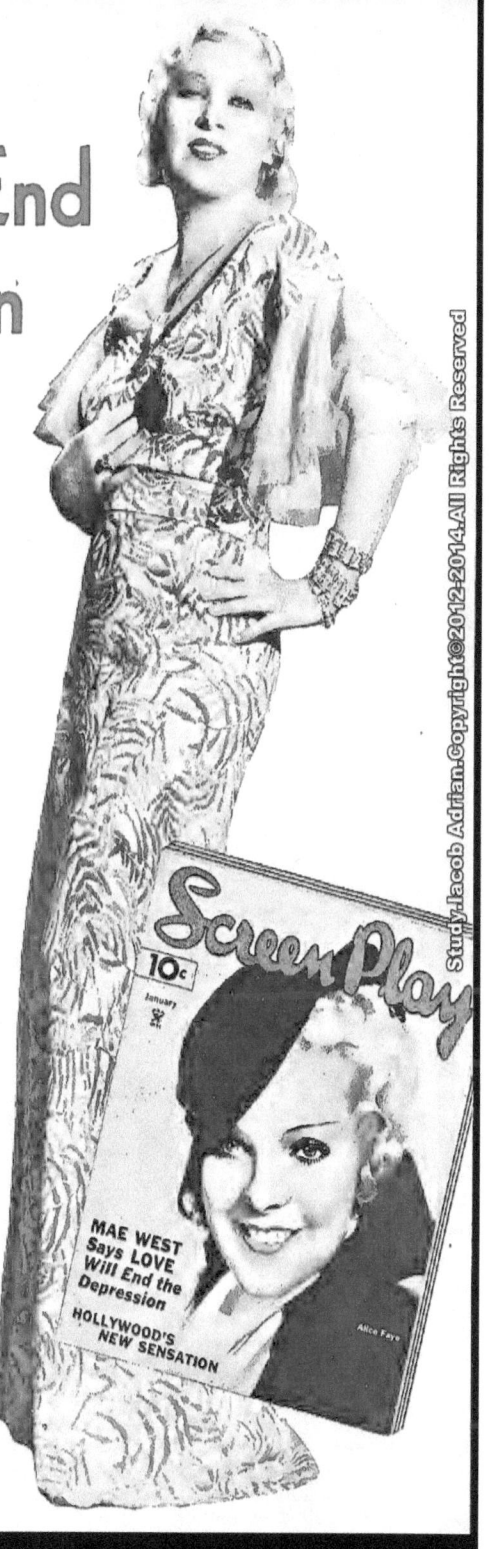

Mae West says
LOVE Will End
the Depression

Mae has it all figured out in a way that is logical and interesting. She knows the public and knows its reactions and she lets you in on the secrets of her reasoning.

Do You Inspire
ROMANCE?

Every girl or woman wants to inspire romance. But how many do? Hollywood's stars have found the formula and they have given it to Grace Mack so that she can pass it on to you in the January issue of SCREEN PLAY.

The January issue of SCREEN PLAY is one of the most interesting movie magazines ever published. It is full of bright, newsy stories written by your favorite Hollywood authors—it has the greatest assortment of fine pictures—it has the best features found in any magazine.

10c At all Newsstands

Get Your Copy Now
JANUARY

Screen Play

Drop me a line

Off the screen, too—as her letter proves—Mae West lightens her earnestness with humor

Bill Cox,
307 Harrison Avenue,
Oklahoma City, Okla.

Dear Bill:

Thanks for all the kind words. Those are the sort of words a woman appreciates.

I'm glad you liked "Belle of the Nineties" and I'm even more pleased that you liked my leading men. Kinda liked them myself. Or maybe you didn't notice that?

I've got another good one for "Now I'm A Lady". His name is Paul Cavanaugh. He isn't had much experience, but working with me ought to be an experience. Acting experience, I mean. He's some good.

Drop me a line sometime.

Sincerely,

Mae West

He Champions Mae West
$10.00 Letter

DEAR MISS WEST:
I am a young boy sixteen years of age and attend the movies regularly. I have seen all of your pictures and can truthfully say that I don't think your pictures are cheap and vulgar, as described by some of these men and women who criticize the movies.

I just saw *Belle of the Nineties* and I enjoyed it immensely, but it is a shame they had to cut out so many good scenes. In spite of that, I saw the picture twice. I want to give you credit for picking such splendid leading men.

Hoping to see you soon on the screen in as good or better pictures, I am
Yours truly,
BILL COX,
307 Harrison Avenue,
Oklahoma City, Okla.

Ann Harding—Inspiration
$5.00 Letter

DEAR ANN HARDING:
For some time, I have wanted to write you and tell you of the interest with which I have followed your career.

You wouldn't remember me, I am sure, but I was just starting my high school education at East Orange when you came there to finish yours. I remember you when you were in a few of my classes, and the very efficient way in which you finished everything you undertook. I remember the class play, in which you had a leading part, and I also remember the seriousness with which you took your rôle in that show. You had so much poise and acting ability, even at eighteen, that you made the other boys and girls in the show look like kindergartners, instead of high school seniors.

I've watched your advancement from the small part you played in your first New York show until you became one of the stage's leading actresses; and from your first motion picture up to the present time.

There is no career which shows more clearly to the American boys and girls the heights which one can attain. There is no better lesson in the will and determination to make something of oneself, no matter what difficulties may arise, than that which you have given to those of us who have watched you from your high school days.

It has taken not only a great actress to succeed as you have, but also a fine character and understanding. I hope that you

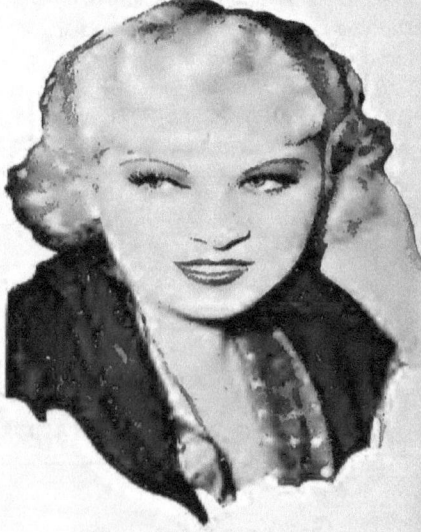

will stay in the movies and not return to the stage, as so many more people can see your work upon the screen than ever could on the stage, and I know that you will continue to give us the fine performances you have in the past.
Sincerely,
ELEANOR D. HINES,
17 Oxford Street,
Newark, N. J.

The New Stream-Lined
MAE WEST
by SUSAN HARTWELL

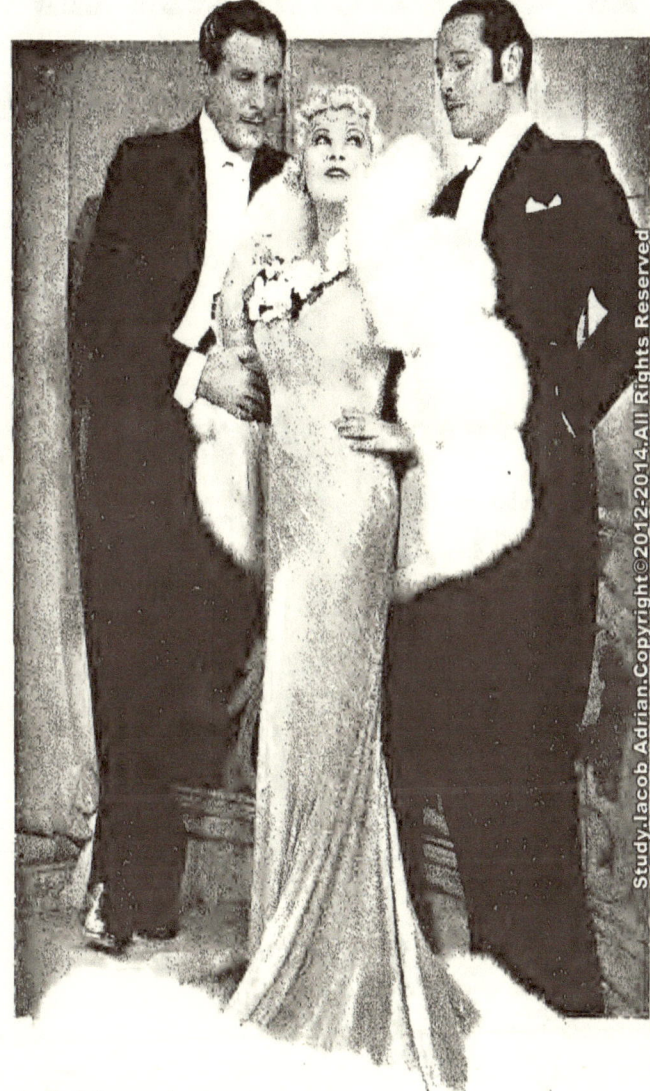

Just a brief two years ago Mae West changed the feminine contours of the world when she swept across the cinematic heavens in "She Done Him Wrong."

Now the versatile Mae is about to do the same thing again, to the delight of the fashion designers and her legions of feminine and masculine fans. But this time she's offering a stream-lined silhouette instead of the full-rounded curves of two seasons ago.

It's all part of the radical change in the character Miss West portrays in her newest Paramount Picture, "How Am I Doin'?" No longer is she a swaggering gal of the Gay Nineties; this time she is the personification of the spirit of 1935. The Westian curves are still there, of course, but they are streamlined in the modern manner.

And the story and background of "How Am I Doin'?" offers just as much contrast to her previous vehicles as the Mae West of 1935 does to the Mae West of 1933. The fashionable spots of smart, present-day society—Long Island, N.Y. and Buenos Aires, Argentina, for instance—replace the Bowery of the Nineties and gay spots of New Orleans a generation ago as the setting for the action of her new picture.

Even her leading men have undergone a radical change. Gone are the prize-fighters and gamblers of an older era; instead honors are shared

by Paul Cavanaugh, suavest of suave Anglo-American actors and Ivan Lebedeff, ace of the heel-clicking, hand-kissing, heart-smashers.

So watch out for the New Mae West. She is going to set a new standard in entertainment, in wise-cracks, in fashions and in the feminine form divine when Paramount's "How Am I Doin'?" reaches the screens of the world.

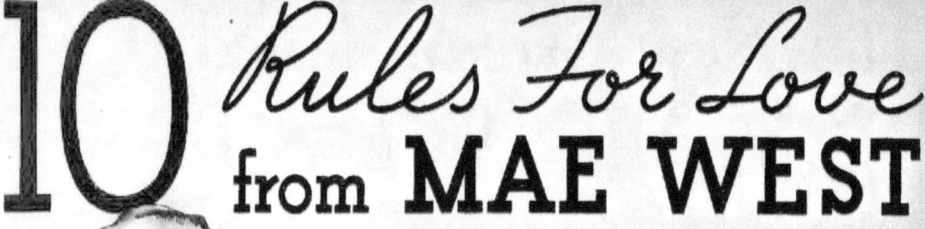

10 Rules For Love from MAE WEST

Gloomy Gusses and all unmarried people beware!
This intimate article is hilariously dangerous

By MADELEINE MATZEN

Mae's Rules for Love

1. DON'T hang out the "Hands Off" sign! "Danger—Men At Work" is better.
2. DON'T economize on clothes! Cleopatra in gingham never would have made her mark . . . or anyone else.
3. DON'T let him know you're smart! Be smart enough to keep him guessing.
4. DON'T be too dumb, either! An empty attic never attracts anything but bats.
5. DON'T be too domestic! It's all right to be a helpmate but don't hang over a kitchen stove while your mate helps himself to someone else.
6. DON'T wait on him! The woman who runs errands can't hope to run a man.
7. DON'T be afraid to know more than one guy at a time!
8. DON'T diet! A curve isn't the shortest distance between two points . . . but it's more interesting.
9. DON'T cheat! Cheaters never prosper.
10. DON'T rake up the past!

If ANYONE COULD give you good, practical advice about holding that man of yours it would be Mae West. She's common sense personified. No fantastic notions tucked under HER pompadour! Calls a spade a spade! From her you get the truth at all times . . . and let the blushes fall where they may!

"I'm told," I said, "that you think a woman in love is stupid? When she's trying to land or hold onto her man she generally does the very thing that will send him flying in the opposite direction? I hear, too, that you said, 'NO WOMAN NEEDS TO LOSE THE GUY SHE WANTS!' Is it true? Come clean! Don't hold back anything!"

Mae grinned . . . that gamin grin of hers.

"Sure, it's true! Men are all alike . . . you've heard that one before. It's a saying as old as God so it must be so. I've doped it out this way. . . .

"If you're in love . . . quit pretendin' to be what you ain't! DON'T hang out the 'Hands Off' sign when all the time you want to be grabbed and held tight. Don't pull the old gag about never having been kissed . . . it'll make a regular guy run a mile! To men, competition is the spice of life!

"DON'T be afraid to spend money . . . especially on clothes! Men never fall in love with economical women . . . and this includes the Scotch. The wife who keeps her husband's nose to the grindstone making money for her to spend on chiffons and lace . . . holds her husband. He'll complain . . . sure! But he'll stick! No man enjoys holdin' an armful of scratchy calico when he could hold an armful of soft silk and chiffon. Would you?

● "IF You'VE gotta mind . . . DON'T let him get wise to it! Laugh at his jokes if it kills you! Hide your mind under a swell permanent or a henna rinse. Men don't like 'em clever and evasive. They like 'em dumb and obligin'!

"On the other hand DON'T be too dumb! Act as though you know enough to come in outa the rain. Let him see you can read the French words on the menu . . . if you do he'll figger you've been out before.

"Graduate from the kitchen! There's a restaurant in every block. Don't try for those pies like mother NEVER made. Go places with him. If your face gets as red as a beet hanging over the kitchen stove it's ten to one he'll go stepping with someone else . . . someone who doesn't know the difference between a frying pan and a roaster. Could you blame him?

"Let him

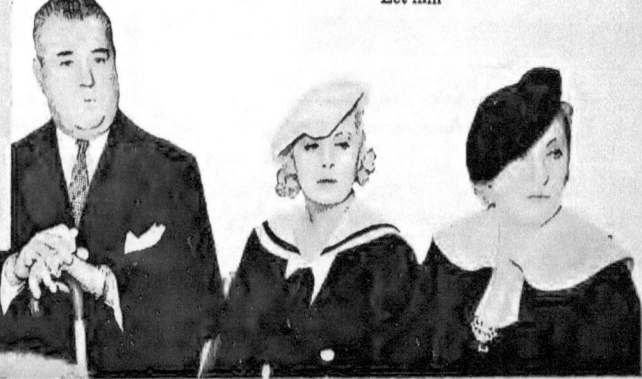

Three familiar Hollywood figures attend a sports event together! Mae West, center, is seen with James Timony, her manager and sister, Beverly West

10 Rules for Love from Mae West

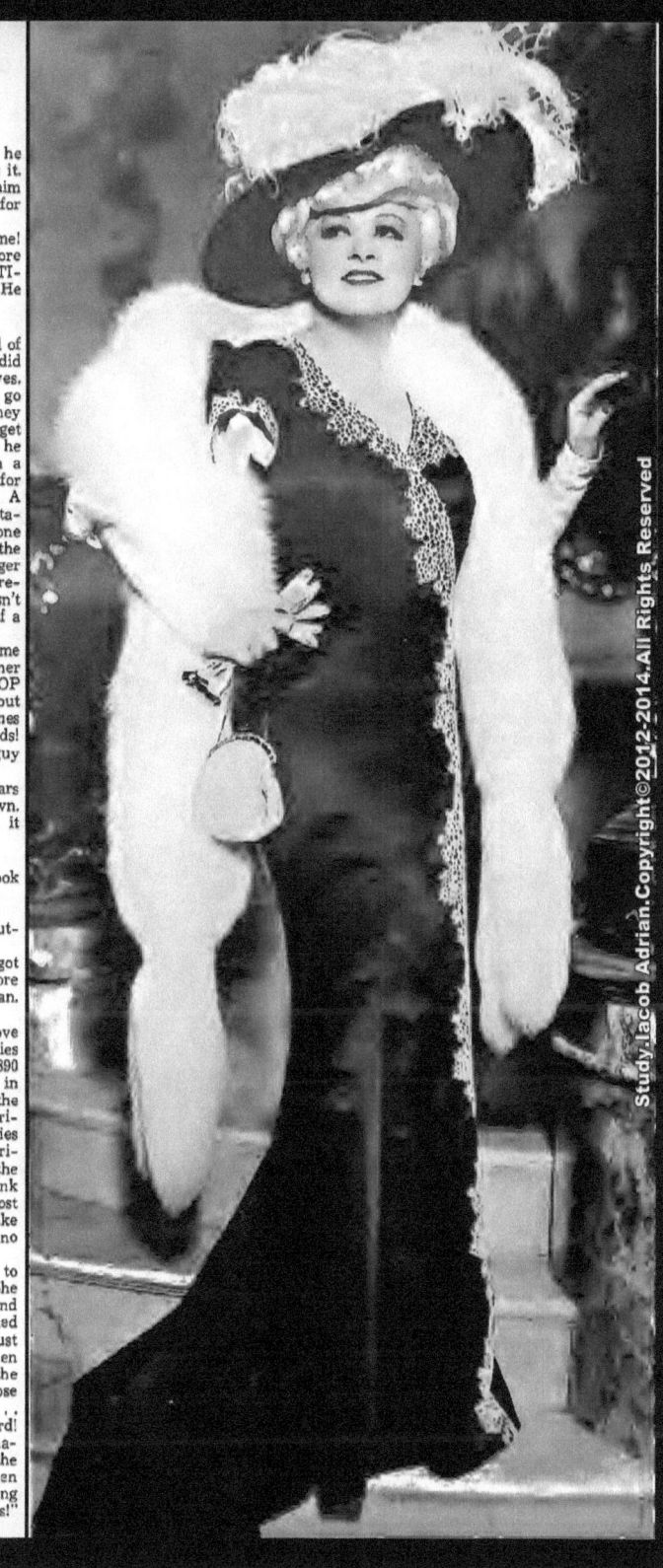

hustle around for you! The more he fetches and carries the more he likes it. The minute you begin to pamper him he'll begin to pout and look around for someone else.

"Know more than one guy at a time! Keep a flock of 'em around . . . the more the merrier! Remember . . . COMPETITION! He'll get jealous? SURE! He loves being jealous!

● LAY OFF the diets! Don't be afraid of gaining a few pounds. I never did meet a fella that didn't like curves. Curves and a good-natured disposition go together . . . they're easy goin'! They don't holler and nag if cigar ashes get spilled on the new parlor rug, or if he forgets to scrape his feet outside on a muddy day, or if he has a passion for thick steaks and mashed potatoes. A dieting woman won't eat mashed potatoes and it gets her goat to see anyone else enjoying them. Nothing interests the dieting one so much as keeping her figger . . . not even keeping her man! But, remember, I said 'curves' . . . that doesn't mean humps or bumps in the shape of a coupla spare tires!

"DON'T two-time! Play the game straight or don't play it at all! Keep other men for a background . . . but STOP RIGHT THERE! I don't know why, but a jane that cheats at love becomes declassé, like a man that cheats at cards!

"Leave the past alone! What a guy don't know doesn't hurt him!

"What happened last year, or five years ago, is nobody's business but your own. You couldn't make him understand it anyway!

● MAE PAUSED for breath and to look around for approval.

She was met with a stony silence.

"Axioms of the nineties!" someone muttered . . . maybe it was I.

"The gal of the nineties generally got her man . . . and held him! That's more than you can say of the modern woman. Look at the divorces!" she retorted.

"I take my nineties seriously . . . I love 'em. Other stars who played in stories of the nineties didn't! I dressed my 1890 gal beautifully . . . they dressed theirs in ridiculous clothes. They emphasized the comic angle . . . the result . . . a caricature! A tin-type! To me the nineties were the most glamorous period in American history. I tried to put some of the color of that time into my plays I think the women of the nineties were the most fascinating women in the world. Take Lillian Russell for instance! There are no Lillian Russells today!

"The gal of the nineties dressed to please men not to please herself. She wore ruffles, trains, big plumed hats and carried parasols and amethyst-studded gold mesh bags. She had hips and a bust and was proud of 'em. She rustled when she walked. She left a FEW things to the imagination! Sex was a mystery in those days and women typified the mystery . . . their femininity was their trump card! Today NOTHING is left to the imagination. Consider the advertisements in the magazines! The bathing suits! Women have become sorta sexless! It's getting harder to tell the girls from the boys!"

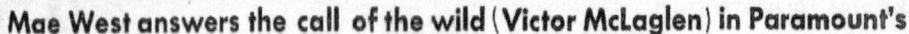

Mae West answers the call of the wild (Victor McLaglen) in Paramount's

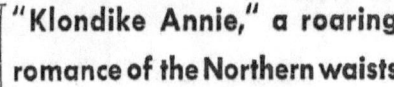

"Klondike Annie," a roaring romance of the Northern waists

You Sleigh Me, Big Boy... Nome was never like this 'till Annie hit town ... these sourdoughs were just a bunch of cheap skates before Annie broke the ice ... but now ... there's a hot time in the Yukon tonight!

Annie Doesn't Live Here Anymore... Tears spout from hardened orbs of Barbary Coast boys as Annie gives 'Frisco the Golden Gate and sails for the wide open spaces of the frostbitten North.

The Big, Bold Miner Stakes His Claim to Annie's Heart of Gold... But Annie can't see him for (gold) dust ... he's just one more fur-bearing animal to her ... the glamour Gal of 'Frisco is not going to give her heart to any lad in a squirrel bonnet. "Get back to the mines," says Annie.

You're No Erl Painting, But You're a Ferocious Monster... Ah, the secret is out ... Annie has given her heart of gold to Skipper Bull Brackett, the toughest lad that ever knocked the teeth out of a gale with a belaying pin. Which proves true love always wins and there's no place like Nome.

Has Mae West Reformed?

Mae West has hit the sawdust trail. Ever since she played the lady evangelist in *Klondike Annie*, the Pleasure Lady of the Screen has been undergoing a noticeable moral transformation.

She no longer visits the glittering night spots of Hollywood.

Her ringside seat at the American Legion boxing stadium has been vacant for weeks.

The beaches see no more of her million dollar curves. She gets her sun tan on an apartment house roof.

Smart shops send clothes and jewels to her suite. She does her shopping at home.

Los Angeles Chinatown is gloomy. She was its most distinguished chop-suey patron. But no more.

Fewer persons are admitted to her apartment. She shuns interviewers.

Even her taste in literature is changing. Once she studied biographies of famous courtesans. Now she prefers books of more uplifting qualities.

She Lived A Role

● For Years Mae Lived the rôle of Diamond Lil, the worldly character she immortalized on the stage and later brought to the screen in *She Done Him Wrong*. It was a memorable performance because Mae, as Diamond Lil, was simply being herself.

Is history repeating?

Did Mae's last screen rôle, that of the pseudo-evangelist, sober her disposition, alter her outlook on life?

Hollywood observers believe so.

There are indications which endorse the theory.

In *Klondike Annie*, as you will recall, Mae played a woman of the world, a glamorous sinner, who donned the solemn raiment of Sister Annie, a gentle evangelist, when the latter died on a strenuous voyage to Alaska.

Mae's purpose in assuming the dead woman's identity was to outsmart police officers hot on her trail with a murder warrant. She succeeded better than she bargained. Not only did she evade the law, but she really began to live and believe in her odd masquerade. The kindly spirit of Sister Annie possessed her and Mae became a tremendous influence for good, a genuine soul-saver in the rough mining town.

Mae loved the character of Sister Annie. She created it in writing the screen story for the picture. She took the rôle seriously, lived it before the cameras. And when the last foot of film had been shot the spell of the lovable evangelist continued to sway the flaming lady of the flickers. Mae had played her part too well.

The Change Becomes Obvious

● Shortly Afterwards evidence of Mae's changed personality and habits made its appearance.

She curtailed social activities.

Curbed her sporting instincts.

Made fewer appearances in public.

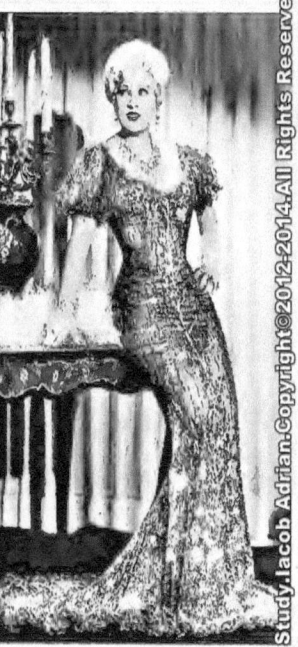

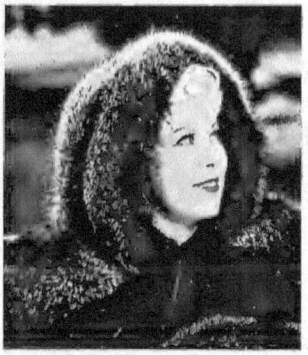

It was while playing in *Klondike Annie*, above, that Mae West encountered a new and potent influence in her life. The oldtime Mae you see below soon changed

Selected more conservative clothes.

Wore less jewelry.

Increased her charitable contributions.

Visited a neighborhood church more often.

More and more, she sought the sanctity of her apartment home high above the seductive night lights of Hollywood.

Like Garbo, she preferred to be alone.

In keeping with her new passion for simplicity and seclusion, Mae makes fre-

Flashing Swords ⟩ ⟩ ⟩ Claude Rains, Louis Hayward

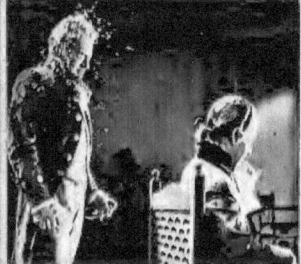

Tense moments from Warners' *Anthony Adverse*. Louis Hayward, as Anthony's father, hurls wine in the face of antagonistic Claude Rains

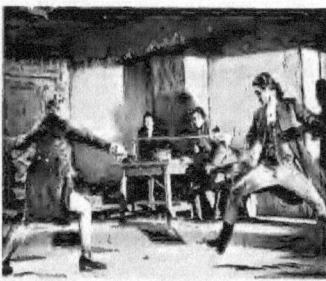

The battle starts! Swords clash on the set as these men battle literally for their lives. One sword thrust tears Hayward's trousers

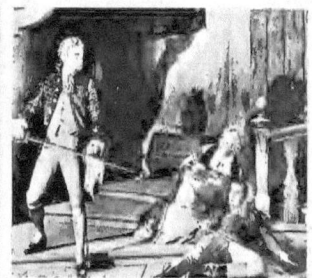

The battle over, Hayward dies as his loved one, (Anita Louise) kneels by him. Thus the birth of Anthony Adverse presaged a stormy life

Has Mae West Reformed?

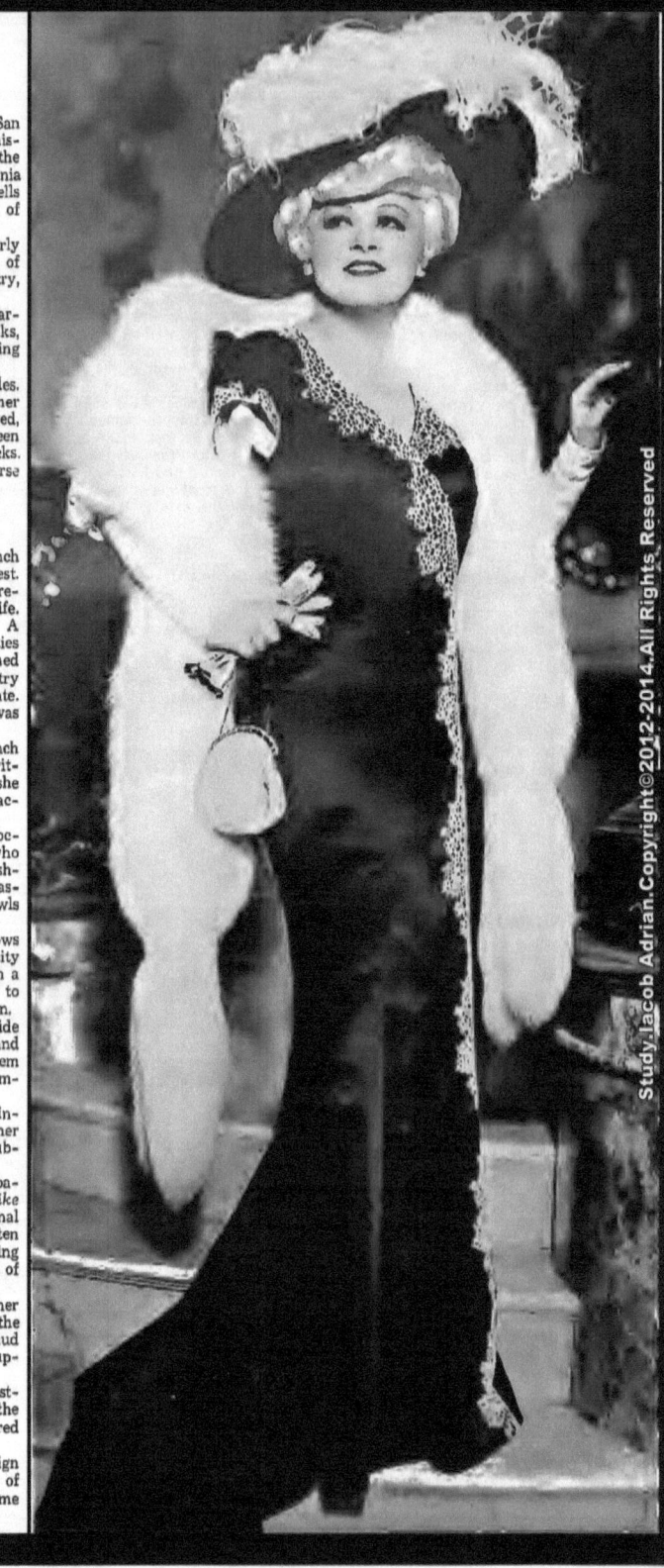

quent pilgrimages to her ranch in the San Fernando valley. Not so far from the historic San Fernando Mission, where the dark-robed padres of early California bowed heads in prayer while ancient bells tolled the angelus, Mae finds a haven of peace and a new love for the soil.

She motors to the ranch in the early morning and puts in full days out of doors. She is proud of her prize poultry, spends hours caring for them.

She has become an enthusiastic gardener. Squatting among vines and stalks, she delights in fussing with growing green things.

She spends but little time in the stables. Conspicuous among the livestock is her brother Jack's racing thoroughbred, Greenspring Lad. The horse has been successful on Southern California tracks.

But Mae has lost her interest in horse racing.

Visits Her Father's Ranch

● MAE ORIGINALLY purchased the ranch for her father, the late Jack West. She had hoped the outdoor life might restore his fading health and prolong his life. Jack was enthusiastic over the place. A product of New York, confined to cities all his life, the genial ex-boxer welcomed the opportunity of becoming a country gentleman. The chance came too late. Soon after settling on the ranch he was stricken with a heart attack and died.

Some say that Mae regards the ranch as a pleasant shrine binding her spiritually to the departed parent whom she adored. Perhaps so. It would be in accord with her new attitude on life.

Mae alternates the ranch visits with occasional calls on her sister, Beverly, who lives in a cozy hillside home in the fashionable Los Feliz district. Here a fascinating vista of all Hollywood sprawls below the wide windows.

Mae likes to sit in one of these windows and let her eyes roam lazily over the city she invaded only a few years ago with a few dollars and a burning ambition to bring Diamond Lil to life on the screen.

Today she has wealth and world-wide adoration. She has sampled fame and riches. Obviously, she has found them empty of the things she now seeks—simplicity and sanctity.

Of course, there are others who maintain that Mae is imitating Garbo in her desperate quest for privacy. It's a publicity stunt. That's what they say.

Insiders insist that the recent newspaper assaults on the picture *Klondike Annie* cut Mae deeply. She took personal pride in the benevolent quality written into the evangelist rôle. It was a stinging jolt to have her sincere interpretation of the character branded indecent.

True, the general public rallied to her support by generously patronizing the picture. But it didn't quite erase the mud slung on an attempt to contribute an uplifting screen performance.

Perhaps the incident left Mae distrustful of her Hollywood acquaintances, the fair weather well wishers, and inspired her present solitude complex.

An interviewer once read a tiny sign in her dressing room: "I can take care of my enemies, but who will protect me from my friends?"

Hollywood's Uncle

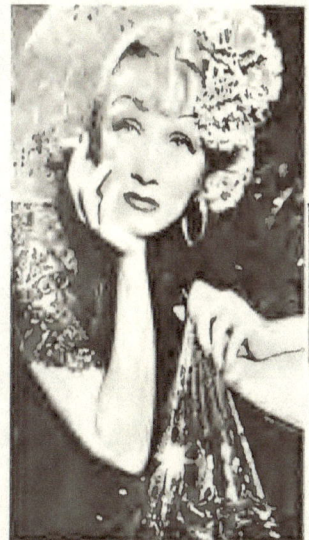

If there's anything of smug happiness in Marlene Dietrich's appearance perhaps it is because she doesn't have to pay Uncle Sam so much as did the blonde on the right

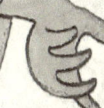

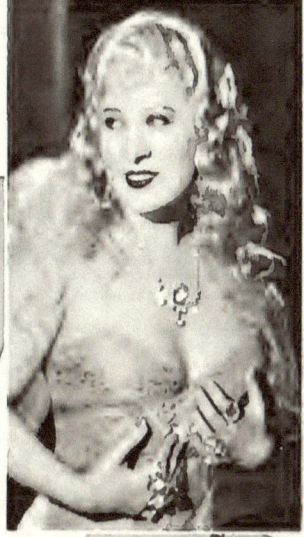

When Mae West cast that "come up and see me some-time" look at Uncle Samuel he went right up and took her for a quarter million. A little boy called "Cal" called too!

Bob Burns, the Arkansas ruminator, has an Uncle Fud. Marlene Dietrich must have a Dutch Uncle.

You remember Universal's Uncle Carl.

And while Uncles are more or less prevalent in Hollywood, there is one old gentleman who Unks them all! He's none other than the one and only Uncle Sam!

Sometimes Uncle Sam reaches for a switch when one of his star-eyed boys or girls displeases him, but as a rule he is well beloved by all, from doll-like little Shirley Temple to our own Mary Pickford.

Just how much of an Uncle is that grand old gentleman who struts about the pages of our newspapers in candy-striped trousers? That is, in what measure does he influence the lives of those of the screen?

We'll just skip over the Home Owners Loan and the PWA (Hollywood has Venetian shades on its poor house) and dive right into the maelstrom of do re mi fa sol.

For a long time there were some of those in Hollywood who thought an income tax lien was something to lean against . . . let's just take a front seat on the steps of the Federal building and watch a real drama of reel people.

Uncle Sam puts on his spectacles and glances at his ledgers. Sighting a cold, blue eye along a straight, hard-knuckled finger, Hollywood's Uncle Shylock suspects that some scores of those in filmdom didn't do their figuring correctly.

"Take a letter," Uncle Shy orders.

Then, a few weeks later he says, "take another letter," talking, of course, to one of his efficient (and how) bookkeepers.

Then later, if nothing happens: "Take one more letter."

When nothing happens then, one of those armrests or liens, which empowers an officer to go out and take anything the unhappy niece or nephew possesses, is brought out and filed.

Then the parade starts.

Let's just glance at the liens filed last year. Is Uncle Sam partial? No. Is he impartial? Yes. Therefore, none escapes? Right!

In these days, 100 liens in a week are not unusual, some of them for huge sums. But Uncle has been in the business long enough to be tolerant and usually

lends an ear and offers a compromise if the circumstances justify it. And in this, he is somewhat different than in the old days.

Seven years ago they would talk indictments and not liens. For instance Tom Mix in his flush days paid more than a million dollars to the government in disputed taxes, interest and penalties.

And Richard Dix and many others paid upward of $100,000 in similar assessments.

Many a sweet young thing who had suddenly come into big money and paid everything but her income tax, had sleepless nights with the haunting specter of prison gates over her.

But although many were indicted, Uncle Sam determined to his own satisfaction that it was the so-called income tax advisers of those days who were to blame and after sending one or two to prison, permitted the galaxy of stars who were haled into court to make adjustments and the indictments were dismissed.

It was Federal Judge Paul J. McCormick who analyzed the situation in the trial of charges against a leading male star with the remark: "We know by experience that actors are poor bookkeepers and must leave these matters to others." And the disposition of that case has acted as more or less a precedent in dealing with subsequent cases.

Since then, taxes have assumed a more prominent part in our national life. The public has been made income tax conscious. Truly, more than ever, the old wheeze about death and taxes is true.

"How much did you have left last year after paying your taxes?"

Now there is a question.

If one knows what his fellow artist made last year, it is easy to determine what was left after the federal government and the State of California passed the hat.

And since Uncle Sam decided to tell all and publish the gross income of the wage earners in the higher brackets, everybody knows everyone's business.

Naturally when Uncle Sam became a tattle-tale, the tongues of Hollywood began to wag.

By
RAY
HANNERS

Hollywood's Uncle

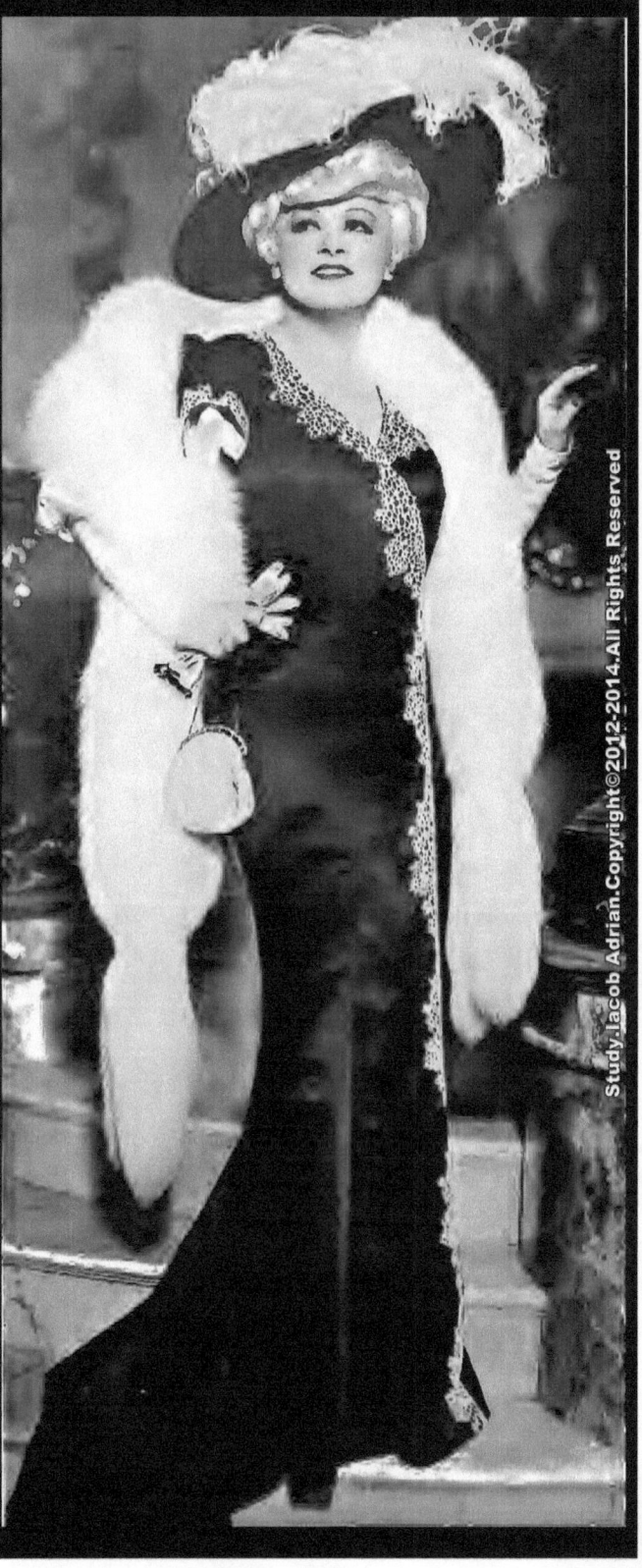

At first blush a lot of folks were plenty mad. Reading in the press that so and so made $50,000 more than you wasn't conducive to harmony. In fact, you were about to make tracks to the front office and holler "robber."

But you didn't. Why? That is the laugh. You got to figuring—well, the more she makes the more she has to pay, and finally you figure out that you made just about as much as she did.

Take Mae West (you might as well, Uncle Sam did). She earned $480,000 last year. But the "Big Boy" went up to see the buxom star and when he left he took about a quarter of a million. Then the little boy (his friends call him Cal.) went up and saw Mae and he came down with some $60,000. As a result Mae had a mere $170,000 left to take care of herself and her retinue.

Now Marlene Dietrich probably was vexed when she saw that Mae grossed $112,000 more in 1936 than she did (as set out in those published figures of earnings). But after the glamorous German actress paid off she found Mae had only about $29,000 more left than she did.

In the lower brackets, while the difference is not so pronounced and startling, it is nevertheless substantial and an efficient healing balm to the lesser grossers.

What will be the effect of this enlightenment? Surely taxes will go no lower. Surely taxes for the greatest earners will increase.

Perhaps next year or within five years the one who earns a half million in a year will have no more left than the one who earns $50,000.

That situation is more than possible. It is nearly a certainty unless those income tax mathematicians figure out a remedy.

All right. What is to happen? To some degree it already has happened. Several stars and high salaried featured players have refused point blank to make more than four pictures a year. In fact more than two have declined to make more than three pictures. And some of the wealthiest, the so-called producing stars, won't make more than one photoplay.

"Give me a good story, expert direction and a large budget and I'll make one picture a year for $100,000," a star will say if he or she hasn't said it by this time. "No, I won't make three pictures for $300,000. Why should I? The government will take most of it and one or even two of the productions might be bad and hurt ME."

Of course, contracts already in force and with one, two or three years more to run, will place the star in a more or less "have to do it" position, but then it may not.

Because the producers also have to pay taxes. Of course, corporation taxes differ from individual taxes. But if you think they are going to be less, stop thinking, these government folks coldly aver. Because taxes have become the greatest equalizer in this modern world of ours.

But behind those critical glances of the government men, there's a warmth of feeling for Hollywood.

Because the film industry has long been one of the chief contributors to the Treasury.

DANGER
CURVES AHEAD!

By
LEW
GARVEY

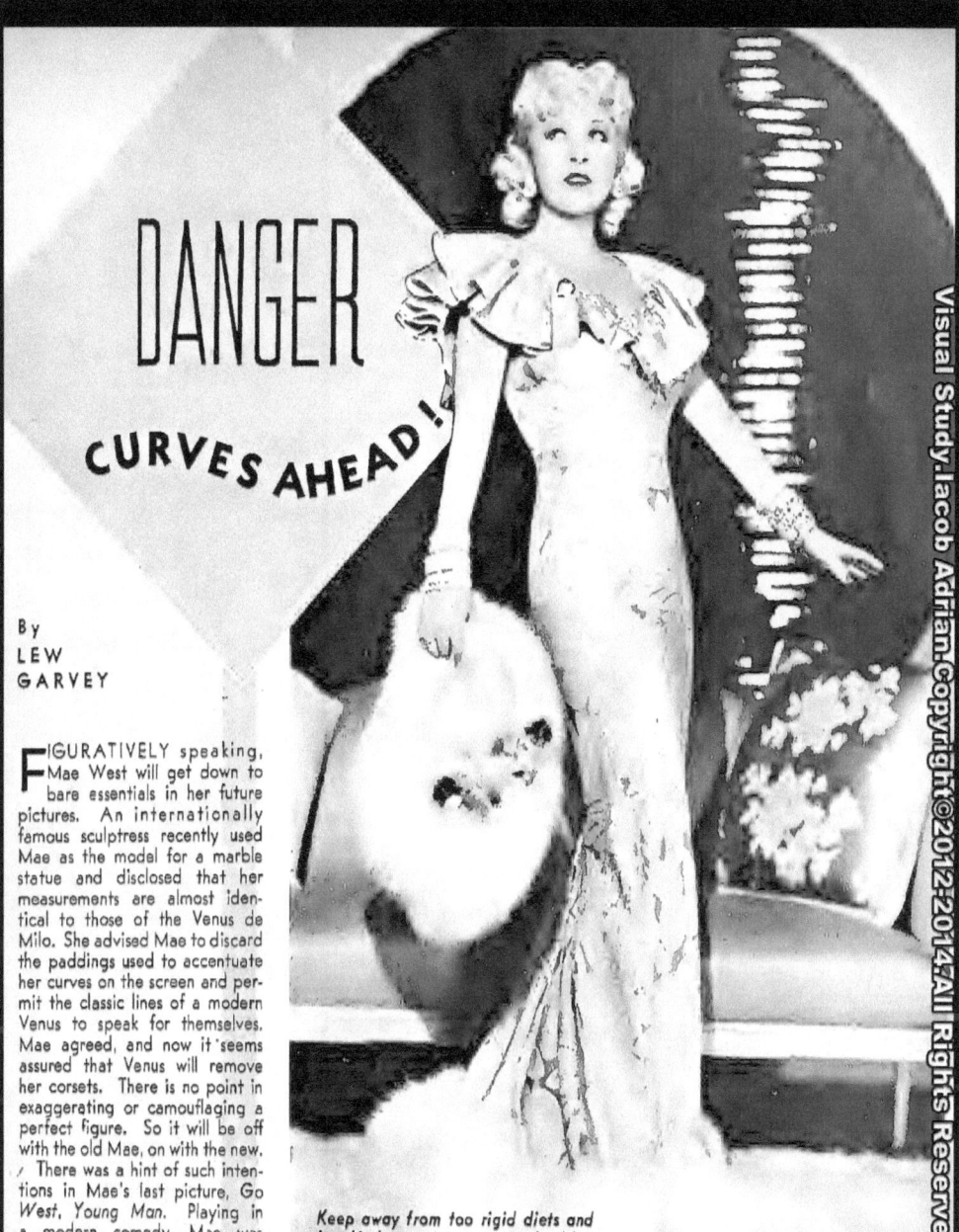

Keep away from too rigid diets and be kind to your curves is Mae West's sincere advice to girls

FIGURATIVELY speaking, Mae West will get down to bare essentials in her future pictures. An internationally famous sculptress recently used Mae as the model for a marble statue and disclosed that her measurements are almost identical to those of the Venus de Milo. She advised Mae to discard the paddings used to accentuate her curves on the screen and permit the classic lines of a modern Venus to speak for themselves. Mae agreed, and now it seems assured that Venus will remove her corsets. There is no point in exaggerating or camouflaging a perfect figure. So it will be off with the old Mae, on with the new.

There was a hint of such intentions in Mae's last picture, *Go West, Young Man*. Playing in a modern comedy, Mae was afforded opportunity to discard paddings and excess apparel. The result proved generally satisfactory to audiences. It emphasized that Mae is equally seductive in 1937 creations or the picturesque vogues of the nineties. Clothes may make the man but in Mae's case an alluring figure makes the clothes.

Mae has another reason for deciding to exploit her natural physique in future screen appearances. Medical men have been voicing protests against the tendency of many stage and screen actresses to practice various trick diets to insure a slim figure. Most of these diets are too exacting and with the desired loss of weight comes loss of health, often permanently. The files of Hollywood physicians are cluttered with case histories of lovely girls who have sacrificed health on the altar of screen opportunity. Unnecessarily so, declares Mae. And the medical profession agrees. If you disagree consider the fact that Mae has banked a fortune by popularizing natural feminine sex appeal on the screen. Income tax figures for 1935 show that Mae received approximately $500,000 in that year alone. Her 1936 income is reputed to be almost as impressive. Such vast earnings, such an overwhelming evidence of public approval, prove that moviegoers

Danger—Curves Ahead!

are satisfied with Mae's voluptuous charm.

MAE'S personal advice to girls is to refrain from too rigid diets. Exercise, yes. But not too strenuously. Don't overeat—and don't undereat.

Mae believes that good figures are born, not manufactured. If you haven't an enchanting shape you can't deceive the public for long with an artificial one. But, if you possess naturally attractive curves, be kind to them. Don't strive to convert them into straight lines. Keep nature on your side.

For several years Mae has been secretly hoping that the popularity of her natural curves and luxurious fullness of form would have a healthful influence on the girls of America. She is gratified today to see this wish coming true. Medical and college statistics indicate that Miss America of 1937 is becoming more interested in a wholesome life, and good clean fun, than a tiny waistline and an anaemic disposition. Women's increasing challenge for supremacy in athletics provides a sound example of the current feminine trend toward naturalness.

EXACTLY how close Mae's measurements approximate those of the famous Venus de Milo may be appreciated from the following figures:

Venus de Milo: bust, $34\frac{3}{4}$ inches; waist, $28\frac{1}{2}$ inches; hips, 36 inches; middle thigh, $19\frac{1}{2}$ inches; calf $13\frac{1}{2}$ inches; ankle, $8\frac{1}{2}$ inches.

Mae West: bust, 35 inches; waist, $27\frac{1}{2}$ inches; hips, 36 inches; middle thigh, $19\frac{1}{2}$ inches; calf, 13 inches; ankle, $8\frac{1}{4}$ inches.

Mae's weight and measurements seldom vary. At least they haven't since she invaded Hollywood. Surprisingly small off the screen, she tips the scales at 122 pounds.

No prescribed set of rules restrict the pleasure-loving lady of the cinema. She eats when she is hungry—and when she's hungry she eats plenty.

IN ADDITION to reviving a vogue for feminine curves and more healthful bodies, Mae has pioneered to an amazing extent in taking the sting out of sex on the screen. By kidding sex, presenting it from a robustly humorous angle, Mae has dealt a death blow to the slinky-eyed vampires and exaggerated sex problems which previously infested screen dramas. Scenario department shelves are crowded with scripts depicting the "stark drama" of faithless husbands being ruined by chorus girls, or wayward sons disowned because of marrying actresses, or shop-girls scorned because the boss bought them fur coats. The studios realize that Mae has changed the public viewpoint on such matters. She has demonstrated the art of treating sex humorously and solving its problems minus tears and torment. Maybe because Mae reverses the dramatic formula in writing her screen plays. Whenever anybody is "done wrong" in her pictures you will note that Mae is on the doing end.

From Gay Paree come additional good tidings for Mae's growing legion of disciples. The world's foremost style creators have issued a call for Mae West type of models.

Meanwhile, Mae continues to reign as the Queen of Figures—physically and financially. The Golden West! That's Mae!

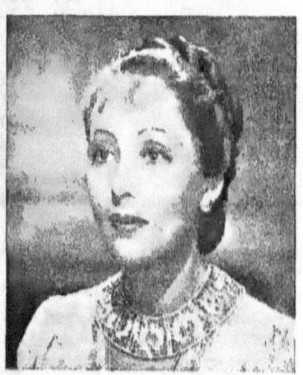 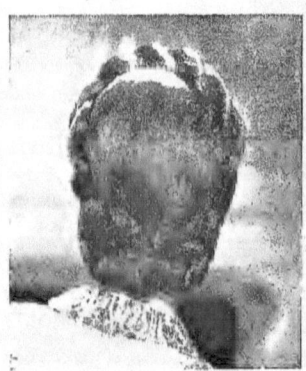

Luise Rainer, M-G-M star, selects this new hair style. The hair is brushed off the face, with the feather bangs and a coronet braid encircling the head. The long hair in back forms a soft roll at the nape of the neck

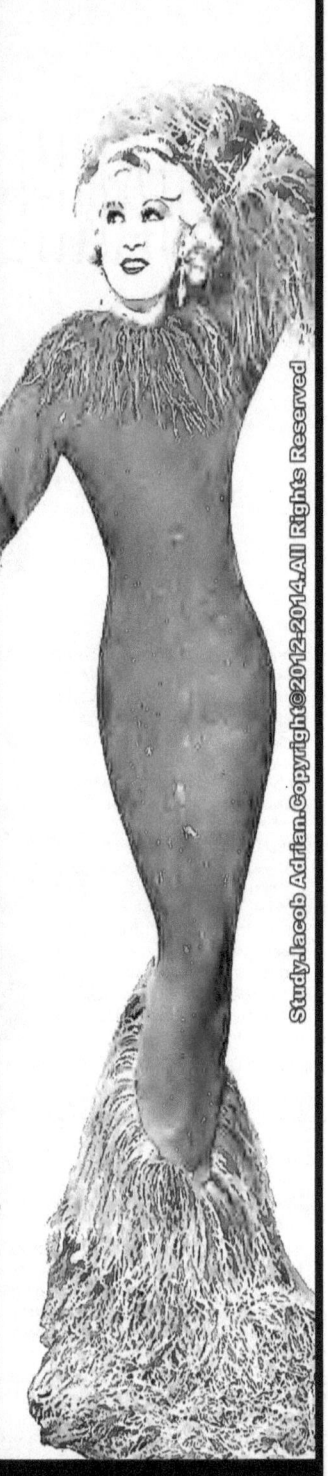

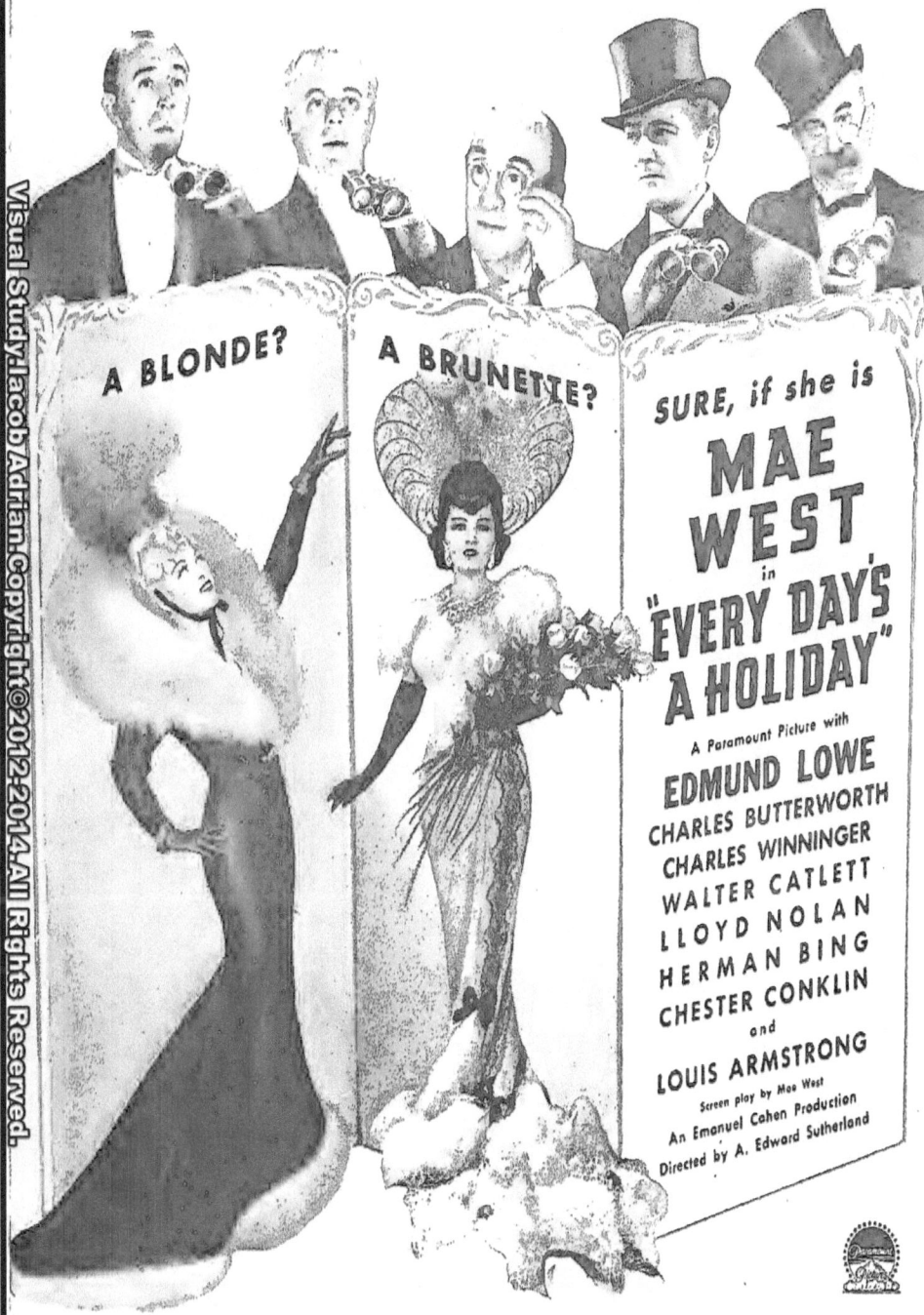

GENTLEMEN obviously prefer...

A BLONDE?

A BRUNETTE?

SURE, if she is

MAE WEST

in

"EVERY DAY'S A HOLIDAY"

A Paramount Picture with

EDMUND LOWE

CHARLES BUTTERWORTH

CHARLES WINNINGER

WALTER CATLETT

LLOYD NOLAN

HERMAN BING

CHESTER CONKLIN

and

LOUIS ARMSTRONG

Screen play by Mae West

An Emanuel Cohen Production

Directed by A. Edward Sutherland

"Every Day's a Holiday" all right when you can see the one and only Mae West herself in a roaring comedy-romance-with-music set in the hail and hearty days of New York's Gay 90's—a gala and glittering picture featuring the antics of five of the greatest screen comics of our time...a picture with the dash of Mae's Schiaporelli gowns—it'll have your boy-friend in hysterics and you in a gale of giggles.

Battle of the Sexes

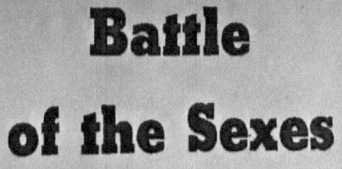

Mae West and W. C. Fields co-starred in *My Little Chickadee* prove that sex is not only popular, it's funny, too

Right, Miss West as the fatal school-marm, Mr. Fields as the great lover

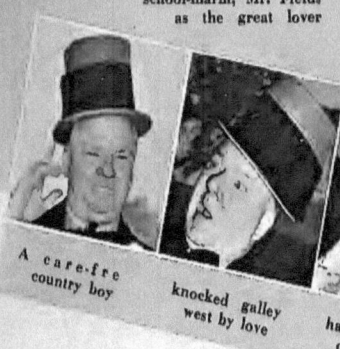

A care-free country boy

knocked galley west by love

has a momen of self-doubt

"After all, I am attractive

"and have a love-ly musical sense

"I can do par-lor tricks, too!"

By THOMAS NORD RILEY

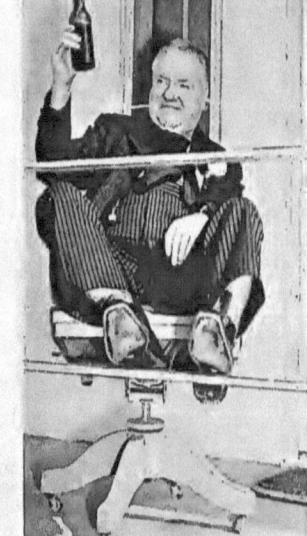

"To the ladies!" W. C. Fields raises the root-beer in salute

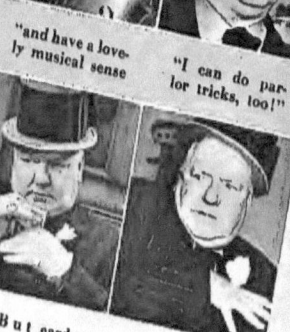

But card-tricks When you want come in handy to forget it all

■ With great bravery, Universal is making a picture called *My Little Chickadee* starring a wicked blond lady named Miss Mae West and a man who will kick a baby in the slats for a laugh, W. C. Fields. If *My Little Chickadee* can sneak through the Hays office without having its innuendoes clipped, the public is in for some hilarity and wild laughter.

This picture is what is coyly known as a super-western and it is replete in scenes calculated to give Mr. Hays and Mr. Breen harrowing existences. Men sneak in and out of the blond lady's bedroom, there is a bogus marriage, a song about man chased by women for the gold in his teeth, Indian fights, and a mob that has its mind set on lynching Mr. Fields for card-sharping.

The Hays establishment has okayed the script, but it is going to look a nervous breakdown in the face just the same, mostly because there is no telling about this blond lady. She is a problem, this lady is. What she's got won't go into scripts. She has the most eloquent gait in the animal kingdom. When this lady walks, scripts burn. Besides that, she has a voice that overwhelms description. Once she read over the air a sweet, innocent-looking script passed by radio censors, and when she finished with it the radio

audience thought they had tuned in on an Elk's smoker. When it comes to saying words the way they shouldn't be said, this lady is just plain breath-taking.

And Mr. Fields, whose nose, like the Dionnes and the Rainbow Bridge, is famed natural phenomena, is no slouch either when it comes to scripts. Mr. Fields ignores them. He is the world's most incorrigible ad libber. It is said that looney-bins are bursting with men who have tried to write scripts for Mr. Fields.

The plot of the picture, arranged especially to present both stars at their best, is the work of

Battle of the Sexes

Mr. Grover Jones. Miss West wrote most of her dialogue; Mr. Fields his. Miss West, as Floradora, a Chicago nightclub singer, comes out west to visit relatives. On the way she is kidnapped by a masked bandit. Later she shows up in Little Bend looking uncommonly contented for a lady who has been kidnapped. That night the masked bandit is observed leaving her room, and the townspeople are perfectly capable of putting one and one together and getting foul play, so they drive Floradora from town and instruct her to get married. Floradora bumps into Mr. Cuthbert J. Twillie, a medicine man with a troupe of Indians, and is delighted to see that Mr. Twillie's carpet-bag is stuffed with money. Floradora decides to get the money by marrying Mr. Twillie in a phony marriage ceremony. Mr. Twillie's attempts to get into the same bedroom with his wife are constantly being frustrated and Mr. Twillie is driven to all sorts of artful dodges to gain entrance. Once he masquerades as the masked bandit and gets in, but Floradora gets a peek at Mr. Twillie's nose and chases him out. Mr. Twillie morosely observes: "I married a woman like the old army game—now you see her, now you don't." Meanwhile, Floradora has fallen for the saloon proprietor, a hard character named Jeff Badger, played by Joseph Calleia, and is absolutely astonished to find she loves both the masked bandit and Mr. Badger. She can't figure it out until she kisses Mr. Badger and in so doing learns that the masked bandit and Mr. Badger are one and the same.

■ As Floradora, Miss West is the one who is going to stab Mr. Hays in the back if he is going to be stabbed, and so we will give you the lowdown on this blonde first, and expose Cuthbert J. Twillie later.

Miss West wears a total of 15 elegant dresses in *My Little Chickadee* and most of them are at least skin-tight. Word has gotten around that Miss West whittled off twenty pounds just before starting this picture. How and where those twenty pounds went has made your correspondent almost intolerably curious, but it is still a secret. What is more vital, Miss West now weighs 120 pounds, and cross my heart and hope to be a purged Russia, if she isn't the toothsomest lady this correspondent has seen since that dream he had about Bali. Her complexion is the make-up man's delight and her eyes are big and blue and loquacious. In other years detractors were wont to say that some of Miss West's lushest curves were swindles, arrived at by using pads, balloons and other unscrupulous equipment, so when Miss West, bulging delicately in a boudoir raiment, swished by for a scene I whispered hoarsely to Mr. Cline, the director: "Am I seeing everything I'm seeing?"

Mr. Cline, who had been directing this blonde for seven weeks then, and still seemed pretty awed, replied: "The camera never lies!"

■ The thing that worried Universal most was the suspicion that the personalities of Miss West and Mr. Fields would mingle like fire and nitroglycerine. Both are members of the old school vaudeville, and it is well known that either of them will resort to anything up to and including murder to prevent the theft of a laugh or a scene. On one occasion Mr. Fields was doing a billiard table act and a comedian named Ed Wynn sneaked under the table and made faces at the audience, arousing laughter when Mr. Fields wasn't expecting it. When Mr. Fields discovered Mr. Wynn he hauled off and pasted him with the butt of the billiard cue and knocked Mr. Wynn colder than a penguin's heel. Such is the stuff with which Mr. Fields and Miss West are made. Consequently, when it was announced that these two would make pictures together, sharing top billing, a localized war was expected. So far, not a shot has been fired.

Each day Mr. Fields greets Miss West with an affectionate kiss on the cheek. The blonde rolls her big blue eyes up at him and says, "Oh Bill, darling; how are you?"

"Fine, my plum, fine. Thank you dear."

"Your nose, Bill," says the blonde.

"My nose, dear?" asks Mr. Fields, caressing his built-in 'cello. "Is something amiss?"

"It isn't as red as it used to be."

"Garcon!" thunder Fields. "Garcon, fetch me my sherry jug, my nose needs conditioning!"

It is an awful thing to say, but I suspect Mr. Fields is flesh and bone like the rest of us, and is susceptible to the wiles of woman. Just after the picture started, Miss West said: "Bill, darling, I don't like the way you're doing your hair."

"Don't you, dear? What's wrong, not enough of it? My mother, Mrs. Dunkenfield, once beheld an Indian scalp a white man. Consequently, I was born bald as an onion. Haven't had much since."

"It's not that, it's the part. Come here, let me do it for you."

It is my humiliation to report that Mr. Fields yielded, let the blond lady part his hair at a new angle, and has worn it that way ever since.

Miss West's solicitude went even farther one day when Fields, clad in pajamas for a boudoir scene, was strolling about the set. Miss West called: "Bill, you must be cold, why don't you put on my robe."

"Mrs. Twillie," said Mr. Fields, "I am a man, not a silkworm."

"Go on, Bill, lots of men wear women's robes."

"And how would *you* be knowing a thing like that, my robust little hourglass?"

"I read it in a book."

■ The actual dialogue of the picture is a secret to be unleashed upon the public undampened by advance reports, but a few lines have escaped:

In one scene Miss West is a school-teacher; a pupil asks: "Teacher, what is addition?"

"Well, one and one are two," replies the succulent scourge of Greasewood City; "two and two are four, and five will get you ten if you know how to work it."

■ As Cuthbert J. Twillie, Mr. Fields is in his legendary role as the man whose philosophy is "Never give a sucker an even break." Mr. Twillie, like most Fieldsian characters, is lovably criminal. Most endearing of his delinquencies is his card-playing, which is adroit and uniformly crooked. He is wearing his gray stovepipe hat in *My Little Chickadee*, palming counterfeit money and managing a medicine show, including an Indian named Milton, played by George Moran. But Mr. Fields, like an anteater, gains a great part of his fame from his gorgeous nose. Your correspondent inspected the livid promontory at close range, and was reminded of nothing so much as of a tomato with hives. This beak of Mr. Fields is worth its weight in radium, for besides being a trademark, it is kind of a nasal pipe-organ from which Mr. Fields delivers sounds ranging from a vibrant snarl to the coo of an adenoidal infant.

As usual, Mr. Fields is ad libbing. He has been ad libbing since an early experience in vaudeville when his partner, a nervous girl, sprinted on to the stage and knocked over a backdrop with a row of houses painted on it. Mr. Fields eyed the carnage, then muttered to the audience: "They don't build houses the way they used to." The audience laughed. After that the girl knocked down the scenery every night.

Sometimes, Mr. Cline, the director, who realizes that Mr. Fields talking on the loose is as good if not better than the script, lets the camera run when the old master has forgotten his lines and is functioning smoothly on what ever comes into his head. Recently, when Mr. Cline was cashing in on these free drolleries, Mr. Fields, without batting an eye, finished out his sentence— "and I'm not saying another word, I only get paid for so much."

If Mr. Hays runs his blue pencil through *My Little Chickadee*, your correspondent is going to join somebody's army.

Mae West's

Cum'up som'time and you'll find the siren from Brooklyn to be the busiest girl in Hollywood

By DOROTHY MANNERS

NEW MOVIE cordially invites you on an eighteen-hour expedition into the private life of Mae West. Mae has what she calls two sets of daily routine "when I'm workin' and when I'm preparin' for it." But recently, just before she put the finishing touches on her next original story, "It Ain't No Sin," Mae enjoyed what might be called a composite day. The plans, the settings and the dialogue are by The One-And-Only, Herself!

6 A. M. "Well, what are you doin' at that hour? So am I! I'm only human . . . some folks say *too* human! Say, is there really such an hour . . . or is it just an idle rumor?"

7 A. M. Mae's apartment. More specifically, her bedroom! Pause a moment to take in the significance of where you are. For no one in Hollywood, with the exception of Mae, and her colored maid, Libby Taylor, has ever set foot in this bedroom before! It is the holy of holies! The inner niche to which neither friend nor foe is allowed to penetrate. In her otherwise untemperamental, placid existence Mae has only one household law: "Keep outta my room! I've got to have some place that's all my own . . . where I can go and shut the door and be by m'self!" This is it! Look about carefully, for this is the first, and last, public inspection of this sanctum.

(A white-and-gold French bed, carefully "pointed toward the north"—one of Mae's many superstitions—is mounted on a small dais. A gold-flecked canopy only serves to accentuate the frilly femininity of the white satin and lace comforter, the dozens of small French

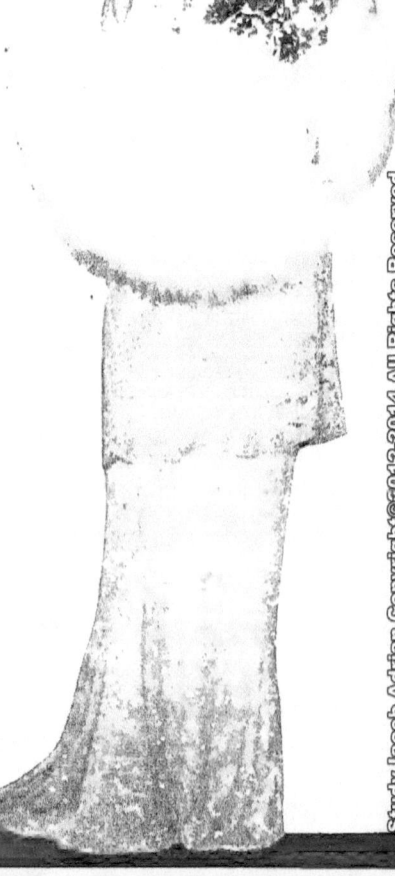

pillows piled together along the foot of the bed. It is the only piece of furniture in the room that belongs to Mae. The rest is typical, but smart, apartment furniture. A pale blue satin chaise-longue, a dressing table sparkling with crystal perfume bottles, a night stand with a modern white lamp and also certain pencil-marked pages of the script of "It Ain't No Sin" on which Mae has worked late the night before. Notice there are no cigarettes or trays about. Mae does not smoke or drink, and so there is no smoking done within the walls of this coral-draped domain.)

8 A. M. Enter Libby Taylor, smiling, buxom, colored, almost stiffly fresh in her gray uniform and starched white apron. Remember Libby as the singing, dancing comedienne maid of Mae's "I'm No Angel"? She was right in character in that role—because Libby is Mae's own personal maid in private life—"an' finest friend" (Libby is always quick to add, "an' finest friend!") Be it known that, though black, Libby was not born into a life of service. Far from it! She was a well-known actress herself on the Broadway stage until it came home to her that she loved Mae more than she loved ambition. Not for any other person in the world would Libby have given up her promising career for personal service. But that's the way Mae gets people. By writing parts for Libby into her shows and pictures she's made it possible for the genial gal to have her cake and eat it, too.

Here is the inimitable Moe, dressed for a Hollywood opening. "Can you imagine me in gingham?" she asks. "What's the matter with velvet or satin, if you're the velvet or satin type?"

Perfect Day

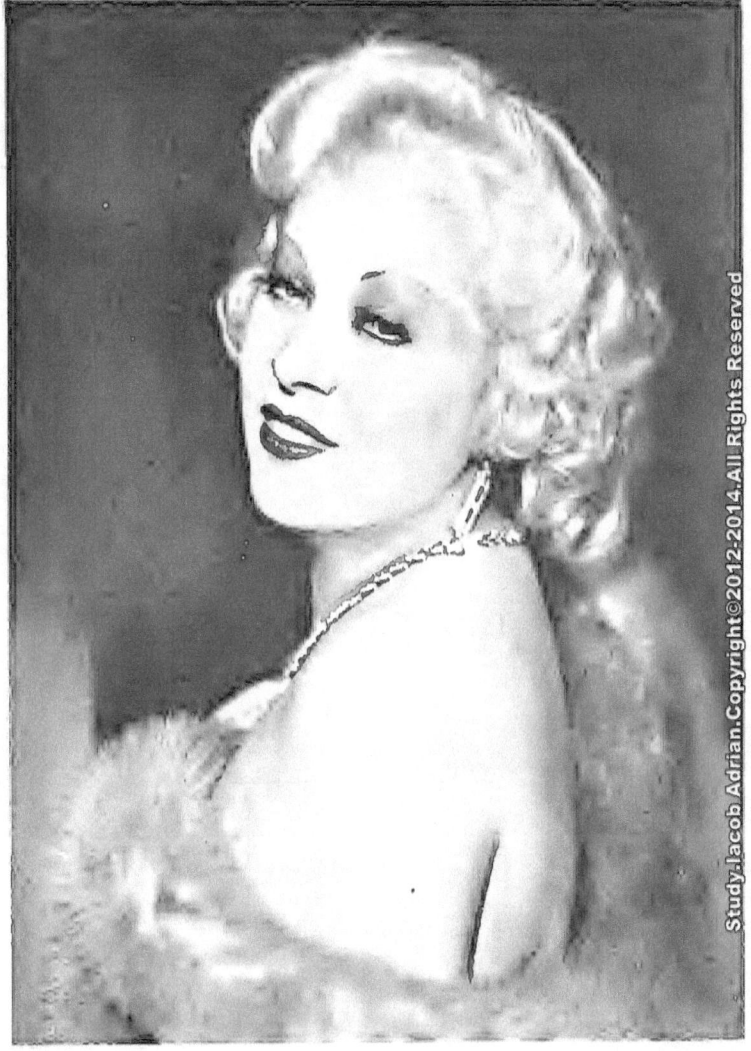

Mae, with her beautiful white shoulders, says, "Me suntanned? Waman's greatest weapon is her snow-white skin. The sun's swell far invalids, but I'm na invalid."

The night "I'm No Angel" was premiered at *Grauman's Chinese* Libby attended, back stage, gloriously bedecked in yellow velvet and gardenias.

Libby runs a tub of hot water into which she generously sprinkles both bath salts and Sweet Pea toilet water. No cold showers for Miss Mae, you bet! Two large, fluffy white towels are stacked neatly on an orchid colored stool beside the tub. A large box of Sweet Pea bath powder and a feathery puff are made convenient before Libby's "pre-waking Miss Mae" activities are completed. Now she stands beside the white-and-gold bed in which a woman with unbelievably white skin is sleeping in a white satin night gown. Sometimes it's blue satin, or flesh satin, but it is always a nightgown—never pajamas! "Bath's ready,

Miss Mae," says Libby softly, "time to get up."

The woman in the bed awakens almost immediately at the sound of the words. "I never know a lady to wake up as easy as Miss Mae," Libby will tell you, "Sometimes you figure she couldn't have been asleep at all." She smiles at the beaming colored woman holding a white velvet dressing gown and white velvet mules. Waking up in a good humor is a habit with Mae. She says: "What time is it?" Says Libby: "A little bit after eight!" A look of blank astonishment settles over the West features. "What's the idea? There's no call today!" Libby, who well knows her mistress does not arise until nearly noon on non-working days, nods in agreement: "I know, but last night you told me you had

Mae West's Perfect Day

a ten o'clock story conference with Mr. LeBaron today." "Oh, yeah," says Mae, remembering.

9 A. M. A bridge table has been set up in the living room near the divan that looks out toward the Hollywood hills. The table is set with a half grapefruit, a low bowl of Cecil Brunner roses, two morning newspapers and several magazines just arrived through the mail. A colored man in a white jacket (no relation to Libby) is dividing his time between the breakfast table and a blond girl busy attaching a hair dryer to an electric plug. As Mae enters the White Jacket drops everything to make a bee line to the kitchen and the beauty parlor operator pauses to greet her famous customer. "Had your breakfast? Well, I'll only be a minute, then we can get to my hair." White Jacket brings French toast with strips of bacon, marmalade and coffee with cream. The beauty parlor blonde is interested. "You don't diet, Miss West?"

"No," says Mae, "I eat what I want. If I notice I'm gainin' a little I get hold of a trainer and exercise it off. My weight hasn't varied in three years. I just tipped the scale at 122 pounds!"

Mae doesn't eat much. The little blonde gets to work almost immediately. There is to be no shampoo, only a "set." As the wave begins to take form Mae keeps up a running fire of conversation and daily orders to Libby:

"IS my brother, Jack, up yet? (Jack has an apartment adjoining Mae's.) Call my trainer and tell him not to come today, I'm busy on a story conference. If Mr. Timony (Mae's manager) doesn't call before I leave tell him I've gone to the studio and I'll see him later. And check with the publicity department about those portraits I'm supposed to make this afternoon. About that interview appointment, I don't know whether I want to give any more interviews or not. I've talked so much for publication I'm sick of readin' it myself." The card table has been cleared and its surface is now occupied by a make-up mirror, a box of face powder and a lipstick. With only casual glances into the mirror, Mae applies her street make-up. If it was a studio make-up Libby would apply it.

"You don't go in for suntan, or the dark powders do you Miss West?"

"Me? *Suntanned!* Say, honey, woman's greatest weapon is her snow-white skin. The sun's swell for invalids, but I'm no invalid!"

In the bedroom, where she's putting out Miss Mae's clothes, Libby Taylor nearly rolls with laughter. But even in her mirth she does manage to select (from a closet jammed with clothes of a like nature) a long, black velvet dress with a white collar, a short white broadtail coat, sheer black stockings, a small black turban with a nose veil. You'd have to be a keener searcher than Libby to find a sports costume in Mae's wardrobe. There just aren't any, as Mae so aptly puts it: "What's the matter with black velvet or satin in the morning, or any other time, if you're the black velvet and satin type?"

9:45 A. M. (a very private interlude). A woman in black velvet and a white coat steps out of her town car and quickly into the doorway of a little

vine-covered Catholic church. *Mae West is not a Catholic!* But she finds peace in church! Peace and a moment of meditation.

11 A. M. For an hour the black town car has been speeding out toward the wide expanses of the Pacific Ocean. Orange stands, the Old Soldiers Home, funny little pink and blue houses come tumbling after one another to the view of the man and the woman on the back seat. This is not a regulation story conference between star and production supervisor. But it's Mae's variety. When there's something serious to be talked over, Mae drives it out. The same pencil-marked script that had been beside her bed is now in her hand. She flips over the pages reading parts of the action and dialogue as she goes along. ". . . . and so I'm dancing in this scene with the General. I'm wearin' a very low, decollete gown—very low, y' understand? The General's front is all covered with medals, big ones with points. As he draws me closer in his arms I look up and say 'General, do you have to wear all those medals?'" The supervisor of "It Ain't No Sin" laughs. "We don't know yet who will be in the cast," he says a moment later. "Maybe not," retorts La West, "but I do. I never wrote a scene or a bit of dialogue in my life that I didn't have some particular actor in mind. I couldn't work if I couldn't visualize in advance the actor who is goin' to play the role." LeBaron looks surprised. Surprise and amusement are apparently his chief reactions to this two-hour story conference on wheels.

1 P. M. A drug store not far from the Paramount Studio. Mae at the soda fountain counter on a stool! While the rest of stellar Hollywood lunches smartly at the *Brown Derby* or the *Vendome* Mae goes in for a bowl of "the best chili and beans in town" at a corner drug store. Except for the soda jerker who serves her this repast two or three days a week the stray customers do not appear to recognize her. "Working today, Miss West?" the "jerker" politely inquires. "Nope," says Mae, "I'm playin' hookey. I'm going shopping with an old friend. Next to breathin' I'd rather shop!"

3 P. M. For two grand and glorious hours Mae, and her Old Friend from Broadway days, have been on a shopping spree through smart, expensive *Bullock's Wilshire*. Mae wouldn't want the Old Friend, or you, or anybody to know, but there's been considerable system to her shopping today. For instance, in the dress, coat, lingerie and glove departments Mae just couldn't find anything *she* particularly wanted, but there was always just the right thing for the Old Friend. Things haven't been breaking so well for the Friend, if you know what I mean. She would protest she really couldn't afford to accept such things, the prices and everything, to which Mae just answers: "Oh, that. . . !" At the perfume counter Mae happened to remember there was a kid in the Paramount offices who was just crazy about Sweet Pea perfume same as she was. A bottle is ordered! And let's see. Oh yeah! Charlie's kid needs a new coat now that winter is coming on. And Anna's mother is in the hospital. Why wouldn't she like one of these quilted

robes? "My!" breathed the Old Friend, "Don't you ever buy anything for yourself when you go shopping?"

4 P. M. The studio dressing-room. Like her bedroom, the color scheme here is white-gold-and-coral. When Mae is working the pretty little three-room suite is her home. She has even slept here after a long siege of night work. A card table offers testimony she has had many meals in the small white sitting room. It is really her favorite family gathering spot. As her car rolls slowly along "Dressing Row Avenue" (one of the two permitted within the studio gates—Mae's and Marlene Dietrich's) she notices that Libby Taylor has arrived, aired the rooms, and placed long-stemmed tea roses in a white vase. "Tired?" Libby inquires affectionately, as she begins to spread make-up goo over Mae's white skin—the portrait sittings are in order.

TIMONY, the ever present manager, arrives. So does her brother, Jack. Timony has many things to discuss, things as far in advance as Mae's contemplated trip to Paris, her long personal appearance tour which is scheduled to follow "It Ain't No Sin." Jack has spent the entire day looking over property in Brentwood and Beverly Hills, for Mae is California minded. She wants the first home of her life to be here. Jack has seen a house he thinks she'll like. "Can it be done in French? I mean can it be furnished in the pastel colors and satin-y things I want?" No, it turns out the house is Colonial. "Out," says Mae. And it is. "Can you imagine me, gingham version?" "What do you want?" inquires Jack, kiddingly, "a chateau?" Mae says: "Well, somethin' like it!" Timony's secretary enters to remind her she is dining with Dr. and Mrs. Harry Martin (Louella Parsons) that evening. And, so, the portrait sitting which is really the reason for her being there, is somehow worked in.

6:30 P. M. The Beverly Hills home of the Martins—one of the few places where Mae accepts invitations. An early dinner has been planned because it is fight night. The popular Doc Martin, head of the coast Boxing Commission, and Mae are great friends. They have a lot in common, their love of the game. At the table they discuss boxers all the way down the line to Max Baer and Carnera. "What I'd like," says Mae, "is to own a couple of fighters. But they won't let me. I hear it isn't a refined business for movie stars!" Mary Pickford, also a guest, laughs. Mary likes Mae. Mae likes Mary. "She says she likes me because I'm so *low down*." Mae kids Mary about that remark. But, as usual, the subject keeps returning to the boxers! "My dad was in the game and one of the best of his time. Lots of people think it's brutal but I've never been able to see how a game that keeps a man on his toes, in the pink of condition, alert, keyed-up, like the box racket, could be considered anything but a darn healthy career for a man!"

8:30 P. M. The Olympic Auditorium, Tuesday night. Mae and the Martins are on time but Mary is not with them. She never attends the matches. As Mae

Mae West's Perfect Day

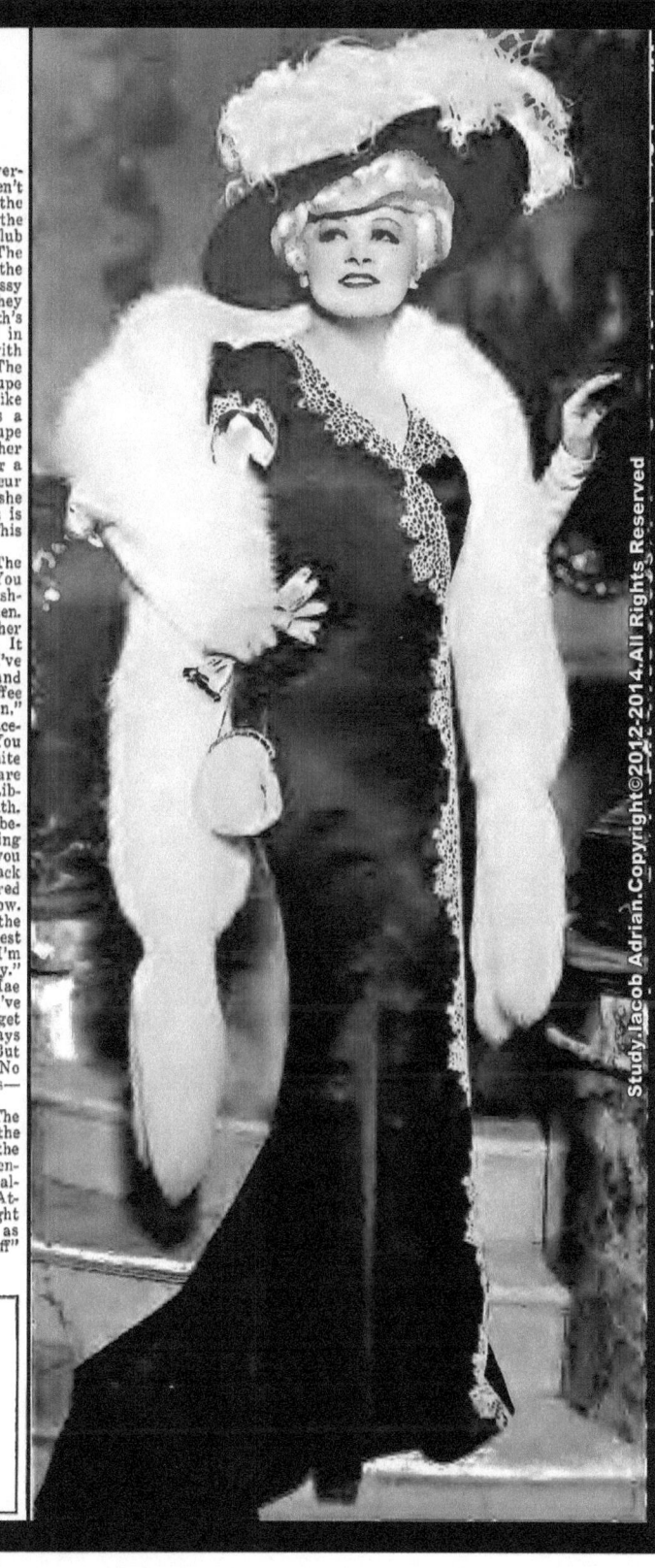

puts it: "We've all got some pet aversions. Now, I hate night clubs. Haven't been in one since I've been on the Coast. As far as I'm concerned the Cocoanut Grove and the Colony Club are just names in gossip columns." The enormous auditorium is jammed to the rafters. The band blares a brassy "The Sidewalks of New York." "They couldn't mean me. That's Al Smith's theme song!" Movie stars packed in like sardines rub shoulders with gamblers, gunmen and gentlemen. The Marx Brothers are there. So are Lupe and Johnny Weissmuller. Lupe, like Mae, loves the fights. But there's a difference in their appreciation. Lupe screams, hollers, whoops it up for her favorite boy. There's not a sound or a move from Mae. She's not an amateur devotee. Only her eyes move as she watches the men in the ring. This is the game she was brought up in. This is her dad's racket.

11 P. M. The apartment again. The devoted Libby has not retired. You know that from the aroma of fresh-made coffee escaping from the kitchen. "Tired?" asks Libby, which is just her habitual way of greeting Miss Mae. It never really calls for an answer. "I've got a nice hot bath drawn for you, and when you're ready I'll serve some coffee while you lie down here on the divan." It's very nice, and restful and peaceful having a Libby in your life! You don't even have to reach for your white velvet robe, or your mules. They are always right there in the willing Libby's hand, as you step from your bath. It's Libby's hands that put pillows behind your back and move the reading lamp up closer to the couch where you are lying. The drapes are pulled back from the bay window revealing the red and white lights of the valley below. The coffee is hot and fresh and the radio plays softly. "I'm going to rest here an hour," says Mae, "and then I'm going to work. You go to bed, Libby." That always begins it. "Now Miss Mae I wouldn't work tonight after you've been out all day. If I was you I'd get a good night's sleep!" "Okay," says Mae because its the easiest way. "But bring me that script of 'It Ain't No Sin' before you leave." Libby sighs—departs.

12 P. M. The radio is silent. The drapes have been drawn against the distractingly beautiful view of the Hollywood valley. Only one concentrated light remains burning, revealing America's Hottest Box Office Attraction engaged in her typical "night life." The pencil pushes on and on as page after page of "Mae West stuff" slips carelessly onto the floor.

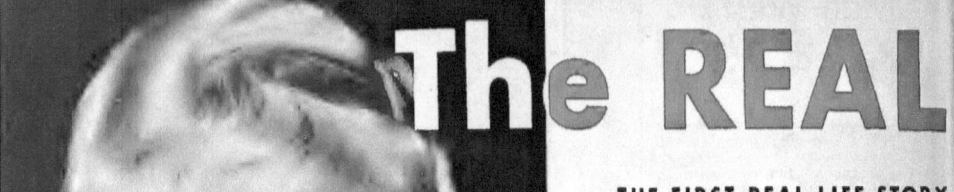

The REAL

THE FIRST REAL LIFE STORY

THE history of motion pictures is replete with stories of colorful personalities who have risen from obscurity to world-wide fame in an incredibly brief span of time, but Mae West is the only one who made herself a star with her opening entrance.

All the others—Rudolph Valentino, Greta Garbo, Marlene Dietrich, Charles Chaplin, Douglas Fairbanks, Gloria Swanson, Mary Pickford, and the late Wallace Reid—served an apprenticeship before the cameras of at least two or three pictures—in some instances, years—but when Mae West, blonde, bold, bad and buxom, swaggered onto the screen for the first time, 20,000,000 people started listening to her song.

The scene showed her checking in at a swanky night club. The check girl admired her jewels.

"Goodness," she exclaimed, "what beautiful diamonds!"

"Goodness," retorted Mae West in that insinuating drawl of hers, "had nothing to do with them, dearie."

Mae West had only a "bit" in that picture, but it was her name that went up in electric lights, and she was the reason "Night After Night" was re-booked in 5,000 motion-picture theaters.

She started an era—the Mae West era. She brought a rowdy spirit to the films, which made Hollywood blush, but which made her the sensation, not only of America, but of Europe, too. She took Paris by storm—fastidious, critical Paris, the rendezvous of the elegant, the suave, la politesse. Somehow, through her utter frankness and honesty, her double meanings are not offensive even to the most sensitive.

She shattered every tradition of the screen as well as the box office, and has contradicted every theory of stardom by her unconventionality, her ribaldry, her boisterous philosophy. She doesn't believe that sex should be taken seriously, but with a laugh. She is unconventional, she says, because Joan of Arc was unconventional, and look at what she did for France.

But unconventional as she certainly is, Miss West, as we shall see, has a code of her own. She has a reason, as well as a wisecrack, for everything.

Mae West's success was not an accident. A lifetime, with all but five years (the first five) spent tirelessly in the theater, lay behind that first entrance upon the screen—years of experience, incessant labor, well-directed energy, firm adherence to purpose

Is she a GOOD OR BAD Influence in Pictures?

MAE WEST . . .

OF THE BROOKLYN BLONDE WHO STARTED A NEW ERA ON THE SCREEN

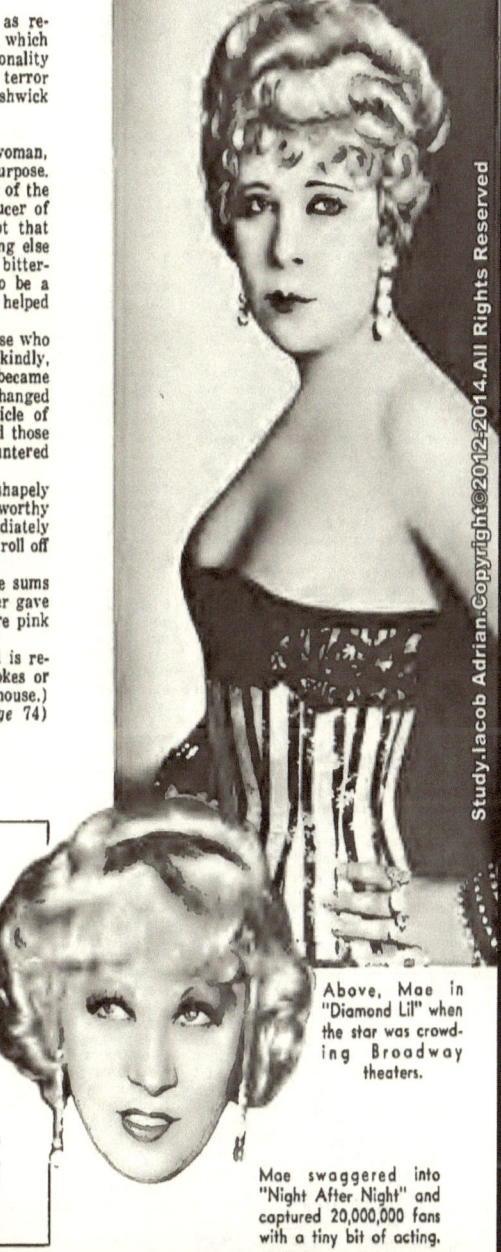

in the face of many discouragements and setbacks, in spite of which she never lost sight of her goal.

Mae West's strong individuality and her firm will are as responsible for her success as her inherent talent—a talent which was as apparent at the age of five as the strong little personality which bossed all the children on the block, and was the terror of the brownstone house district of Brooklyn—the Bushwick Section.

MAE WEST the child, as with Mae West the showwoman, never allowed anything to swerve her from her purpose. During her long career, which has taken her into all phases of the theater, stock, vaudeville, burlesque, musical comedy, producer of her own plays, Miss West, as I said before, never forgot that her aim was to reach the very top. And there is something else she never forgot—something many women do forget in the bitterness of struggle for success. She has never forgotten to be a woman, and it is this warm, gracious quality which has helped her to become the celebrity she is today.

Despite the fact that she is now a world-wide figure, those who knew Mae West "when," and "after," find her the same kindly, unaffected, hard-working woman she was when she first became known in show business. Her success on Broadway never changed her, and her success on the screen has not made a particle of difference in her attitude toward life in general and toward those less fortunate than herself whom she frequently has encountered in her long journey into the various phases of the theater.

Mae West has a level, as well as a clever head, on her shapely shoulders, and I have never known anyone representing a worthy cause to ask her for financial help that she did not immediately reach down into her stocking—which serves as a bank—and roll off a banknote from her wad.

Ostentatious in her love of jewelry, she contributes large sums unostentatiously to worthy causes. The only party she ever gave in Hollywood was for the little orphans at the circus, where pink lemonade and peanuts were the refreshments.

She is a woman of great sympathies, great courage, and is remarkably abstemious in her private life. (She never smokes or drinks, yet being feminine, she's scared to death of a mouse.) Mae West the woman is just as (Please turn to page 74)

BY AILEEN ST. JOHN BRENON

Above, Mae in "Diamond Lil" when the star was crowding Broadway theaters.

Mae swaggered into "Night After Night" and captured 20,000,000 fans with a tiny bit of acting.

Prizes for Your Opinions

What do you think of Mae West? Do you think her influence upon motion pictures has been good or bad? Is she a gusty, invigorating force? Is she a rowdy, damaging influence? Has she helped or harmed the screen? There is no question but that Mae West hit films hard, that her personality cannot be discounted.

NEW MOVIE wants your opinion. For the two best letters in 250 words, answering the question, "Is Mae West a good or bad influence?" NEW MOVIE will pay $25. NEW MOVIE wants the best arguments on each side. Address your opinions to Mae West Contest, NEW MOVIE, 55 Fifth Avenue, New York, N. Y. Letters must be mailed by June 1st.

The Real Mae West

remarkable, just as fascinating a human being as Mae West the celebrity. But totally different and at opposite poles are Mae West the star, and Mae West the woman. And it is the woman as I have seen her that I want to introduce to you.

You all know Mae West the star, whether you live in Hyde Park, London, Charlottenberg, Berlin, or Chillicothe, Ohio. "Take all you can get, and give as little as you can" is the philosophy of Mae West, the celebrity, but as you will see, the philosophy of the real Mae West is "Give where you can, give generously, unsparingly of yourself, of your money, of your time, to your work, to your friends, to those who are weaker than yourself."

It takes more than merely acting to become a national figure—an emblem—which, strange and contradictory as it may seem, is exactly what Mae West is. Fashions, figures, diet, manners, social customs, even morals, as we shall see, have felt the influence of her strong personality.

She was voted by the Seaman's Institute as their favorite actress.

She was nominated a Kentucky Colonel by Governor Ruby Laffoon.

The Central Association of Obstetricians and Gynecologists endorsed her unanimously at its annual convention, whereat Dr. W. P. Holmes of Chicago delivered himself of these sentiments in regard to her Rubens figure:

"If it is Mae West who is responsible for this new, yet age-old fashion, my hat is off to her. The return to plumpness is a boon to motherhood."

A Hudson River houseboat plies the river bearing her name.

J. P. McEvoy, the famous author and humorist, gives public thanks on behalf of writers, for her initiating the new era—an era of wide skirts, full bosoms, ostrich feather boas, large hips, trains, and the ample curve of the "90's"—the Diamond Lil of the stage, Diamond Lou of the screen, Lady Lou to the boulevardiers of Paris.

She abolished the modish repression known as the boyish form, and making sex funny instead of lachrymose, murdered one screen convention after another—and has thrived.

She advised the skinny girl: "What the good Lord has forgotten, we'll put there with cotton," being an advocate of curves because "they will get you farther than an angle."

MAE WEST knows men and how to appeal to them.

She knows, too, that the charm, the romance and the glamour of the Lillian Russell period captures man's imagination. She knows that men, though they flirt and play, and are often caught, to their sorrow, by the wide-eyed ingenue, really love women with charm and poise and worldly wisdom; that men know they are being teased and hoodwinked by their platinum blondes and fall for them, but that they are willing to die for their well-rounded, full-bosomed inamoratas of the "90's".

Men know Mae West the minute they meet her, but she never does a thing to attract their attention. Off the screen she dresses simply—usually in black. But men are attracted, as Cary Grant explained to me, by her intense

human qualities—her love of people, her interest and desire for their welfare. She is frank and spontaneous, utterly unaffected. Moreover, she is considerate and understanding, and very, very witty. Absolutely on the level herself, she's intolerant of sham —and is quick to detect it. Years on the stage have left her no illusions.

Her grasp on life is tremendous and her sympathy inexhaustible. She knows, likes and understands people—sums them up quickly. She is essentially the sophisticated woman of the world who has tasted life with all its experiences. But it has not left her bitter—it has made her big.

Naturally talented and clever, keen and shrewd, Miss West has, since the age of five, devoted all her efforts toward mastering her profession, climbing the ladder of success, as she will tell you with a laugh, "wrong by wrong."

IT is interesting to know, and I will tell you the story later, just why, how and when Mae West decided to be bad—professionally. For the moment, let's meet the high-spirited little flaxen-haired girl, the daughter of the Wests, known because of her unconventional exploits at an early age as "that West child," and looked upon with arched eyebrows by the conservative mothers of the neighborhood because she was, untamed, stubborn little spirit as she was, the leader of the block, she refused to conform to the then current pastime of playing jacks in lady-like fashion on the top step, preferring to gang about with the boys.

Mae West, the daughter of a French mother and an American father, grew up in the Bushwick section of Brooklyn. She was one of those children whom all the neighborhood knows—you know the sort—a forceful little mite, getting into every kind of mischief (instituting most of it), determined to see it through—the sort that all the other children look to for leadership and a jolly good time of it, and the kind grown-ups watch and frown upon.

She became used to the public eye at an early age because she took part in neighborhood theatricals. She was a child actress at the age of five, and strange as it may seem in the light of subsequent events, one of her most popular roles was that of the angelic child of all times, the studiously polite and decorous little being of the velvet suit and lace collar, known to the world as "Little Lord Fauntleroy."

Mae West's mother was a native Parisienne. Miss West says she got that insinuating strut of hers walking over men, but as long as her mother was alive, her daughter Mae accorded her a devotion and a reverence seldom seen in these days of scorn for family ties and neglect in general of the older generation. Until the time of her mother's death three years ago, the two were seldom apart. Miss West went to her mother for advice about her life, for counsel about her work, and for discussion of all the problems besetting an active and strenuous life.

Hardboiled, you ask? After her mother's death, Miss West, prostrate with grief, was unable to see a living soul for days, remaining in her room

alone trying to reconcile herself with the loss of the person she loved most on earth.

But I am ahead of my story. Let's go back to the Bushwick section of Brooklyn, where a clever little flaxen-haired girl lived with her parents. Battling Jack West, the one-time lightweight prizefighter, was her father, and it was from him that she received her first interest in the manly art of self-defense. To this day she is an ardent fight fan. It is one of her few diversions and she never misses a fight, always occupying a ringside seat with "some of the boys."

MAE WEST was a strong, husky child, full of vitality, determination and fire. She explained to me one day that even as a child, once she got an idea into her head, nothing on earth could get it out. "I don't give myself any credit for that," she said. "I'm just that way—so stubborn and difficult once I get an idea into my head." Her mother was the one person in her early youth who had the patience to cope with it.

She tells of a visit she paid at a tender age with her mother to an elderly spinster, very precise and inflexible. In the living room of the elderly lady's house a multi-colored globe on a mahogany table caught the fancy of little Mae's childish eye. Bored by the conversation, she edged her way over to the table and began to finger the bowl curiously, as children do.

"Little girl," said the elderly lady in cold, disapproving tones, "you're too big to handle other people's things. Keep your hands off— you should know better." Something in the woman's tone was too much for Mae's amour propre. She went and found her hat and coat, stalked up to her mother and announced: "We are going home, Mother." Her mother coaxed and cajoled, apologized and threatened. Candy, cake and cookies, even knicknacks, were pressed into service. It was useless—home they went—and Mae, wounded to the heart, never entered the undiscerning old lady's portals again.

Another day her mother took her to the toy department of a store on Brooklyn's Broadway to buy a doll. When she entered the shop, Mae's eyes lit upon a shelf full of matchless beauties with flaxen hair and long, curling eyelashes. On the top of a pyramid of boxes, so high the salesman could not reach them, Mae spied immediately the doll she wanted—a fetching creation in lavender. The salespeople united in trying to persuade her to choose another doll. There were pink ones, blue ones, yellow ones, bigger ones, dolls that talked and walked and cried, but Mae, to the exasperation of the assembled salespeople, was adamant. She could see they all hated her cordially, but she stood her ground. Finally, exasperated, they sent for a ladder from the basement, and a scowling salesman, too annoyed even to pretend to be gracious, got her the doll on top. Ever since, Mae says, she's wanted everything at the top and will be content with nothing less.

When she was about four years of

The Real Mae West

age she began showing an aptitude for mimicry. She appeared at the amateur performances of the neighborhood church and club socials, giving impersonations of Eva Tanguay, Eddie Foy, George M. Cohan and other popular vaudeville headliners of the day. Her take-off of Eva Tanguay, the unrestrained, hippy favorite of soldiers, sailors, college boys and tired business men of that day, invariably won her the greatest applause. It practically gave Mae West her start in show business.

MAE WEST never forgets a friend nor a kindness, and seems to have an inexhaustible memory for the faces of those who have crossed her pathway in her long journey from Brooklyn to Broadway.

Like all the children on the block, Mae West went to the public school, and she passes over the monotony of the schoolroom for the more exciting adventures in the evening when, as a child actress, with grease paint and furbelows, she occupied the center of the stage.

Her first professional appearance took place with the Clarendon Stock Company at the Gotham Theatre in East New York. She was the little daughter who cried out "Father, dear father, come home with me now," in "Ten Nights in a Bar Room." As Little Eva she often took the piano-wire route to heaven in "Uncle Tom's Cabin," playing, as a matter of fact, a large repertoire of child roles in the good old days—"Little Lord Fauntle-

roy," "The Moonshiner's Daughter," "East Lynne" and "Mrs. Wiggs of the Cabbage Patch."

As a member of the stock company, when there were no child parts in the plays, she was called upon to take part in what are known in old-fashioned plays as "olios," or vaudeville acts in between the scenes of the plays. She sang popular songs and gave her imitations, being what was known on the billboards as a "coon shouter." It was at this stage of the game, she avers, that she learned to roll her eyes, a propensity, however, that had to be curbed when she became, for the sake of drama, "Little Eva" or "Little Red Riding Hood."

She continued her schooling, off and on, to please her mother, and when she was "going on twelve," she made another interesting discovery. It was the interest—reciprocated, she admits —she had for boys. She never played with girls at all if she could help it. "Gee, I loved the boys," she says. "Went around with lots of them and played with them. There was a gang of us—of course, we would have fights." And since she was a husky child, she'd smack a boy on the nose as quickly as she would a girl.

Popular as she always has been with boys and men, Mae West has never married and she has very definite reasons why she, who typifies all that is seductive and charming to mankind, has preferred to pursue her career in real life alone.

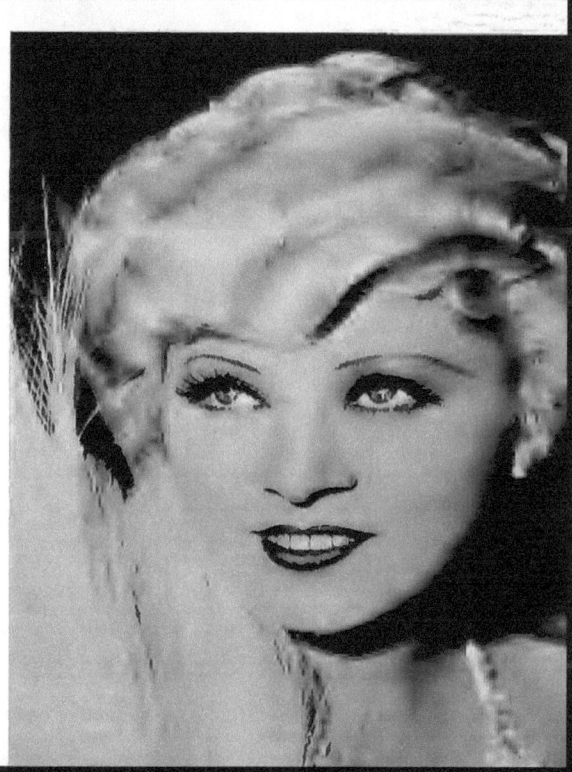

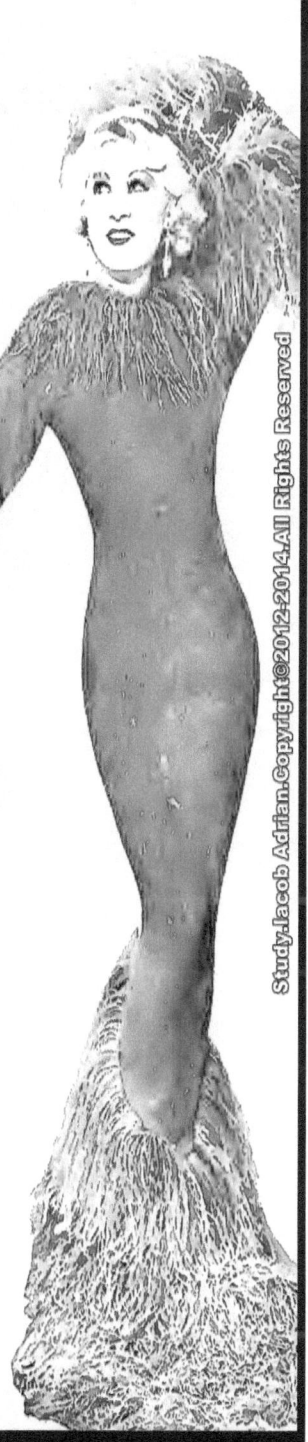

They're the Tops. WHY?

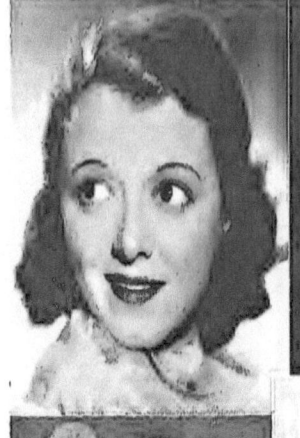

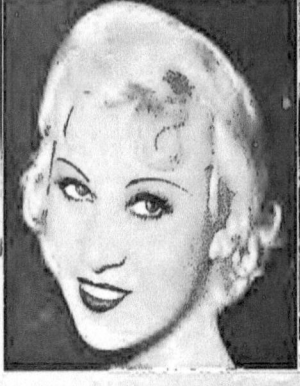

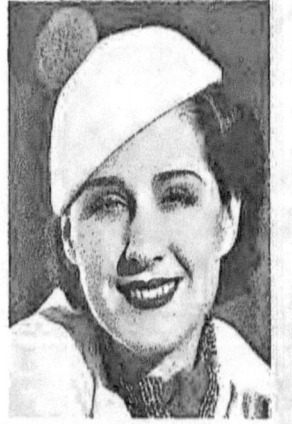

It may surprise you, but box-office figures never lie. These are the five leading women stars. Each one shares the mysterious secret of success. WHAT IS THAT SECRET?

By

JACK JAMISON

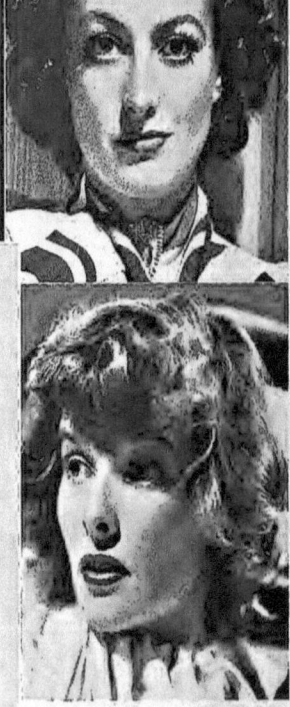

IF someone asked you, "which are the five greatest women stars?"—which five would you name?

Box-office figures never lie, even though they sometimes shock you. The five big women stars today are:

First, Janet Gaynor.
Second, Mae West.
Third, Joan Crawford.
Fourth, Norma Shearer.
Fifth, Katharine Hepburn.
Why?

What is the mysterious quality, possessed by these five women, which places forty million fans at their feet? What do they have, what power, what ability, that lifts them out of the ranks even in Hollywood itself, and sets them over other women stars, as ruling empresses? What is it? If you had that secret, wouldn't you have a prize infinitely more valuable to you than the fabled philosopher's stone, which turned everything into pure gold? Yes; for you would have not only gold, but fame, national homage, success in any profession you undertook. Why, you'd have the very secret of success.

You may not be a scientist or psychologist, you may not have a laboratory, but you have seen these five stars on the screen, you have read their lives. You really know them better, in a way, than you know your closest friends. Why shouldn't you, by carefully comparing them, be able to discover a clue to their secret?

JANET GAYNOR was discovered entirely by accident some years ago when a picture called "The Johnstown Flood" needed a girl who looked boyish and could ride a horse. It wasn't until she made "Seventh Heaven," still her best-remembered film, that her box-office personality came through. It jibed with an image that was in the public mind; that of a helpless little waif, half woman and half child, at anybody's mercy. No one has ever pointed out that the character Janet gives us on the screen is identical with the pathetic little tramp played by Charlie Chaplin, psychologically. Both are wistful, frustrated creatures; bewildered, utterly unable to cope with life. Perhaps because all of us are at heart defeated and bewildered and wistful, this is a character with universal appeal.

Oddly enough Janet fights, bitterly and continually, against the very thing which keeps her one of the Big Five! She's a mature woman, who has been married and divorced. She wants to play mature roles, glamorous roles, sophisticated roles—anything but the wistful waif! Again and again

she tries to break free, only to have her pictures fail the moment she steps out of the characterization in which people are used to seeing her. Sheer pressure of public demand forces her back, again and again. The ironic spectacle of a woman struggling against the one thing which explains her success! For—don't doubt it—if Janet ever says good-bye to that waif, once and for all, she may be dashed down into obscurity overnight!

IT would be a hard job to imagine any greater contrast than Janet and Mae West.

On Broadway Mae's name used to stand for risqué plays. No one admitted it with more alacrity than Mae herself. She wrote her own little dramas, and the critics joined in jeering at them, dubbing them Hokum for Hicks and Bait for Boobs. Yet even with the rural visitors Mae wasn't a success. She never got rich off her New York stage productions.

Compare this with her unparalleled rise on the screen. Wherein lies the difference? Censorship! For there was censorship long before the Decency Drive was heard of, remember. On the screen, from the start, Mae played risqué plays without actually being risqué. It revealed her true appeal, a compelling, dynamic, sweeping feminine vitality that literally knocked us out of our seats. "It isn't the things she says, it's

They're the Tops

the way she says 'em." The lines in her pictures, whether they're routine wise-cracks turned out by Hollywood gag men or her famous catch-phrases, are really no funnier than the jokes in any other picture. It's what Mae herself puts into them. And what she puts into them is—vitality.

There were Mae Wests in ancient Greece. There were Mae Wests living in sod huts on the Kansas prairies a hundred years ago. There were Mae Wests in the days when men lived like wild animals in caves. Hearty wenches, broad in the waist and deep in the chest, who fought beside their men in war, were excellent mothers to incredible batches of kids; who lived, loved and died passionately. They had just what our Mae has today—sheer animal strength. The irresistibility of healthy, pagan, dynamic human fleshliness.

Wiser than Janet Gaynor in the ways of the world, Mae knows what she has and turns it loose to run wild. She doesn't fight herself, she lets herself go. To the *n*th degree, she is herself. That this self happens to be one that is attractive and interesting is just plain good luck.

JOAN CRAWFORD, on the other hand, is caught in much the same trap that grips Janet in such a vicious pressure. No one who knows her, questions Joan's sincerity. She longs passionately to be a great actress, to take whatever roles may come her way and lose herself utterly in them. It is her staggering value as a star name, in terms of sheer dollars and cents, which keeps her from doing it. The business office and her fans, together, force her cruelly to go on playing parts which, after the manner of Horatio Alger heroes, let her rise from rags to riches.

When she tries another pattern box-office receipts and fan letters fall off.

It isn't the money. Joan, despite her new contract, is rich enough now to do whatever she pleases. It is her loyalty that stops her. Loyalty to the studio that took her out of the ranks. Loyalty to her fans.

But others have loyalty. The thing which Joan alone does, which makes her one of the Big Five, is symbolize Youth. In the jazz age she was a dancing daughter. Today, the jazz age gone, she still typifies the modern girl's hopes and dreams. She is the little nobody who becomes a grand lady. Granted that she has verve, beauty, chic, all the rest of it. Others have them, too. But Joan, and only Joan stands for the spirit of our ever-changing younger generation. It is a symbol which will never lose its glamour. Yet—and what bitterness!—she is chained to it!

EXPLANATIONS of Norma Shearer's prominence have been crueller than those suffered by any other star. People react to Norma in no uncertain terms. Either they adore her or they loathe her. There seems to be no middle ground.

Proof, in itself, of an exceptionally powerful personality!

But—"She's a success because she's Irving Thalberg's wife." "She gets people to go see her pictures by playing in polite bedroom comedies flirting with the theme of adultery." An ugly word, adultery. And ugly accusations.

Irving Thalberg is a powerful man in Hollywood. True. If he so wishes, he can give his wife the best stories, the best technicians, an elaborate and costly production. But nothing that Thalberg can do in this world—nothing

—can make people pay their good money at the box office unless they want to see Shearer. As for the other accusation, if all Norma has to offer are bedroom farces, then why were "The Barretts of Wimpole Street" and "Smiling Through" so successful?

No, Norma's appeal lies within herself. It is not the fact that she is beautiful in face and figure. But she is beautiful inside. You sense it. An ordinary Canadian girl, she has lifted herself to social position, financial security, joy in her husband and her child. Given only her own bravery, she has won out in life's battle. The words "ordinary girl" crept into this paragraph, you'll notice. They tell the whole story. Norma—wise, serene, lovely, mature—is Everywoman. Everywoman, that is, plus Everywoman's hopes, aspirations and ideals. Janet Gaynor cannot change her parts. Mae West is too shrewd to think of it. But Norma Shearer could play a Janet Gaynor part one day, and a Mae West part the next, and not lose any of her popularity. She can be any woman because she is—every woman!

WHERE the fifth actress on the list is concerned, prophecies are dangerous. Katharine Hepburn's personality is not yet completely formed. In comparison to the others she is still a newcomer. The others have lasted. Whether Katharine will last it is still too soon to say.

But our concern is to analyze her vogue. Why has she shot up to stardom like the proverbial skyrocket?

First of all, because she is completely unique—an actress who looks different, behaves differently, talks differently.

The clue is in her appearance. Any observant person has seen that same taut, twitching nervous skin in nervous little girls. Little girls, usually, with high foreheads, spectacles, freckles and skinned-back hair. School teachers often call them "problem children." Their brains are years and years ahead of their immature bodies. They are too sensitive. They shrink from rough games, from the antics of their schoolmaster. Quite often they are hysterical, so highly strung are their nerves. Katharine, both on the screen and off, is the problem child grown up. Erratic, unconventional, rude, egotistical, living so thoroughly in an unreal world of her own that she can tell reporters "I have never been married" and really believe it, though everybody knows it isn't true. No wonder she's called wild. Whoever cast her for the part of a half savage, mountain girl, as "Trigger," knew what he was doing!

Katharine Hepburn is one of the Big Five because she is a bad case of nerves.

Thousands of others fail. These five have risen to glory. Notice this—

Each of the five is completely and absolutely different from the others.

Janet Gaynor is sweet . . . Mae West has terrific physical vitality and stark appeal to the senses . . . Joan Crawford typifies youth and romance . . . Norma Shearer is the mature woman of the world . . . Katharine Hepburn, sometimes boyish, sometimes hoydenish, is a steel spring so tightly wound up you think she'll break at any second.

There is their secret. They are the Big Five because, unlike mediocre, unsuccessful people who are "afraid of what the neighbors wil think" if they're the least bit different, they stress, accentuate and even exaggerate their differences! They are individuals.

If you want to take a leaf from their book—find your true personality, dare to be different, and give it all you've got!

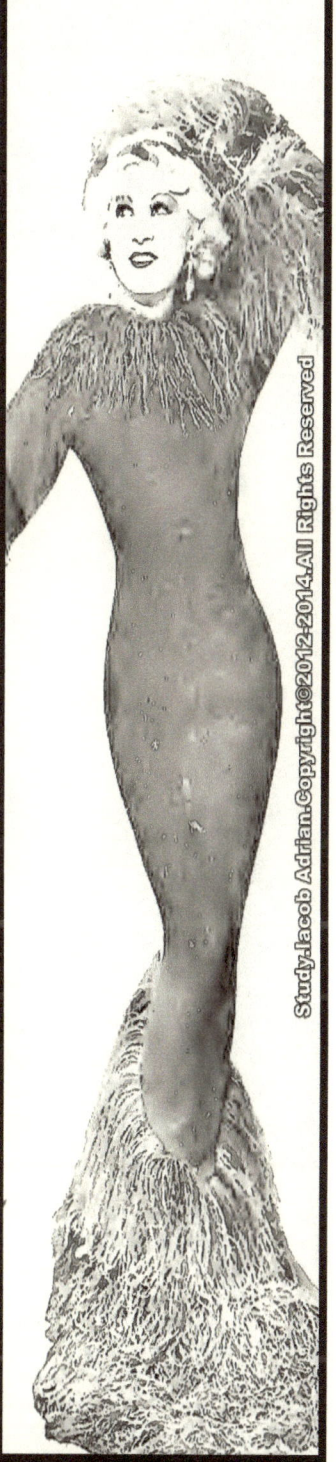

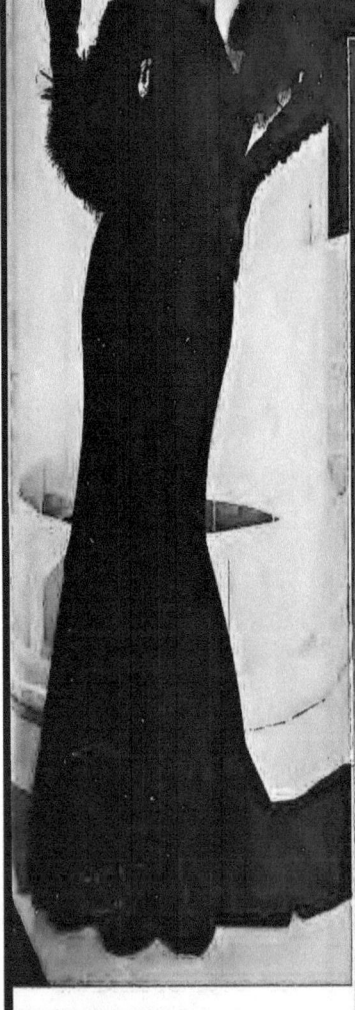

GIRLS
OF GOLD

Bachrach   Zobbm

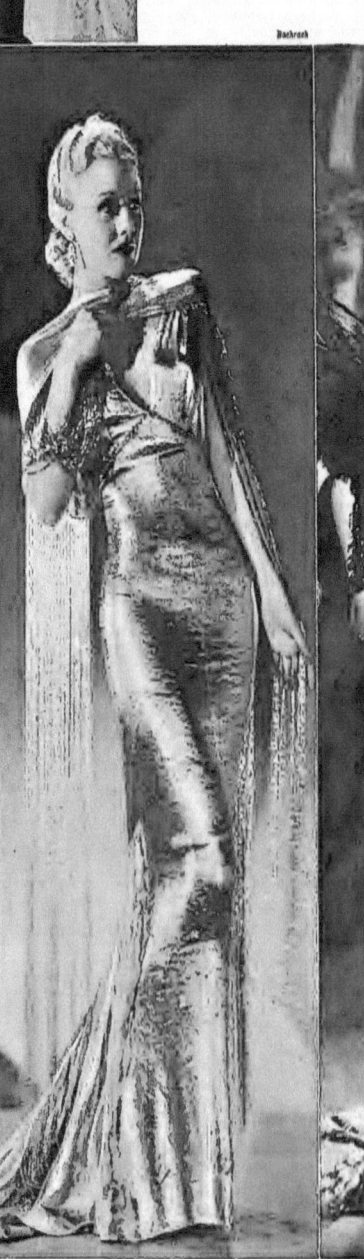

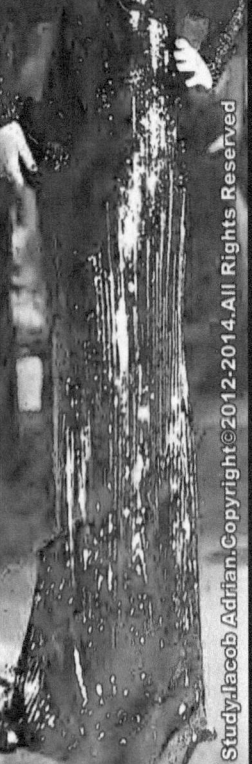

● Above: Lyda Roberti, a siren who hides behind a disarming screen of gaiety, colors Fox's "Scandals" with her own brand of lure. Center: In a gown that is a sheath of cloth-of-gold, piquant Ginger Rogers floods "Roberta" with her most dazzling glitter. Right: In sequins and black paradise feathers, Mae West goes thoroughly modern as her svelte self in "How Am I Doin'?"

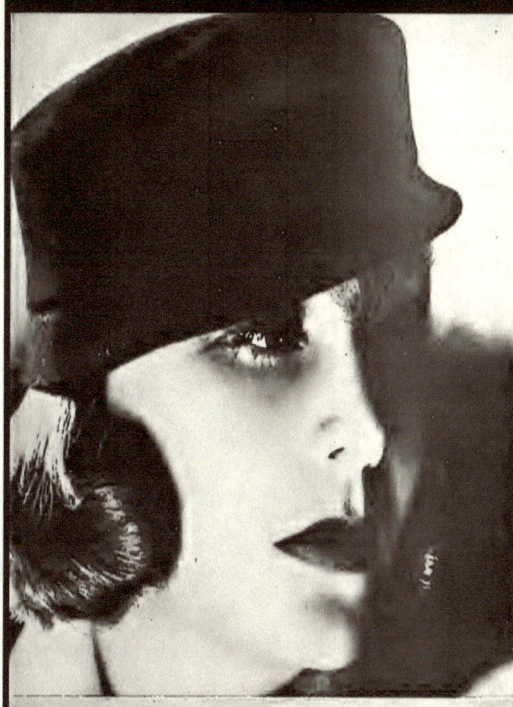

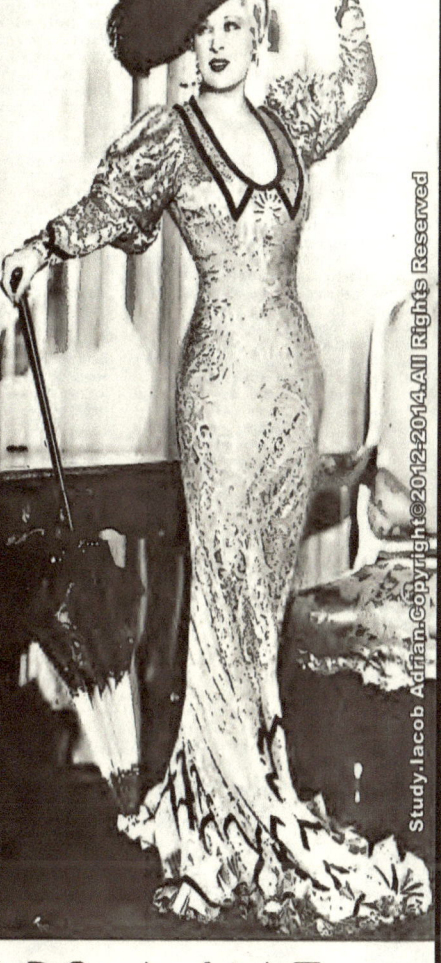

No matter how silly the hat, if Garbo wears it a new style is set. Mae West, at the right, brought back curves to millions of curve-less women. Katharine Hepburn started a rage for frou-frou bangs, Joan Crawford's leg-of-mutton sleeves swept the country and Kay Francis' generously exposed back was a shock heard 'round the fashion world.

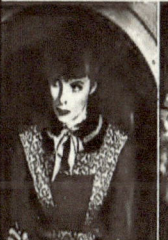
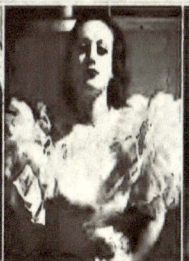
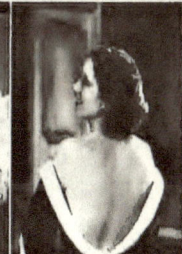

IF GARBO WEARS A HAT

By

WHITNEY WILLIAMS

THE Hollywood influence is felt 'round the world.

Fashions, manners, romance, everything that affects the people of the globe . . . all have been swayed by the screen and its glittering stars.

There is, for example, Joan Crawford, who re-clothed the girls of the land by the way she wore a dress.

It featured leg-of-mutton sleeves.

Who else but Joan could have started this old style anew, in "Letty Lynton," a style that experts for years have declared as dead as mutton? Yet, when Joan wore the dress, millions of girls all over the country rushed to the stores and dress-makers to order one, puffed sleeves and all, for their wardrobes.

To Greta Garbo the women of the world are indebted for the low bob. The Swedish actress came into prominence when most of the stars were cutting their hair short. Despite remonstrance from every expert in the studio, she refused to cut her hair like the others. Shortly after she appeared on the screen with this style of haircut, those girls and women who couldn't grow their hair fast enough were tacking on shoulder-length extensions.

Hollywood has been designated by many the style center of the world. Actually, it isn't (as yet) . . . and its fashion designers lay no claim to this distinction.

But the effect it wields on current fashions, through the vehicle of the screen, is undisputed. Many of the styles and fashions of the day, now so much in vogue, can be traced directly to Holly-wood and its glamorous personalities.

The Cossack hat which Marlene Dietrich wore in "The Scarlet Empress" may be mentioned as a case in point. Shortly after this picture was re-leased, the market became flooded with Russian chapeaux, all outgrowths of the Dietrich top-piece.

The muff she carried was responsible for the re-appearance of that feminine adornment.

And the hood on her cloak is seen this year on all the smart evening cloaks in the smartest shops.

Three pieces of feminine finery now popular throughout the country and in some sections of Europe . . . each had its creation, for general use, in one picture, a film that did not enjoy any par-ticular success at the box-office but exerted a very definite influence upon the styles of today.

Going back a few years, and not so many, at that . . . feathers became popular following the showing of Miss Dietrich

If Garbo Wears a Hat

covered with them, literally, in "Shanghai Express." Travis Banton, who designs all the costumes seen in Paramount pictures, executed her outfit to be in keeping with the character she portrayed . . . and was amazed when he discovered he had popularized feathers and boas once more.

One of the best-known designers in motion pictures, Banton designs gowns, slippers, hats, et al, not with an eye to their setting new styles, but for the sole purpose of the stars' being atmospherically correct when they wear his creations in a picture. He received a shock the first time he ever saw one of his gowns reproduced in the mode of the day . . . and it is a never-ending source of astonishment to him to know that his fashions are constantly setting new trends in feminine attire.

The flowing draperies of the new gowns, jeweled collars, sandals, negligees, feathered turbans . . . these fineries of the moment are directly traceable to the costuming of Claudette Colbert in "Cleopatra."

Mae West set a new style—or should I say a revamp of the old?—in her wearing of the hour-glass costume in "She Done Him Wrong." The effervescent Mae also brought curves back into popularity.

Kay Francis' bare-back gown in "Jewel Robbery" established that vogue, since found modified in many ways . . . and the tunic dress Jean Harlow wore in "The Blonde Bombshell" has been widely copied by designers the country over.

R EMEMBER the silly little pill-box hat Garbo donned for "As You Desire Me"? It immediately created a demand for hats of this order. Shirley Temple and Baby Jane dresses have been on the market for some time, each a copy of a little dress seen on these starlets in one or another of their films. And, believe it or not, four of the dresses designed for "Little Women" are featured this season by a famous Paris gown shop, exact replicas of those old-fashioned styles. For the first time in history, the smart women's magazines are offering their readers elaborate layouts of new styles glimpsed on the screen.

The influence of motion pictures on fashions may thus be clearly seen. Fashion experts throughout the East acknowledge this without hesitation, and even from far-off London assenting voices may be heard.

Victor Stiebel, whose styles now are the rage of the English capital, on a recent visit to Hollywood confided that his journey to the cinema center meant at least ten thousand dollars additional each month to him. More women than ever would patronize him, he said, when he announced that he had made a personal study of some of the best-dressed women on the screen. Conclusive evidence, this, of the truth of the above paragraph.

And before we continue . . . Lily Dache, noted millinery creator of Paris and New York, while she, too, was spending several weeks in Hollywood studying the fashions of the studios, became so intrigued with the clothes worn by Miss Dietrich in "The Devil Is a Woman," latest picture of the German star, that she told Travis Banton she planned copying some of the hats that will be viewed in that film. High praise, again, for Hollywood and its fashions.

W HENEVER a feminine star changes her hair-dress, immediately thousands of inquiries pour into the studio, asking for news on this new style of coiffure.

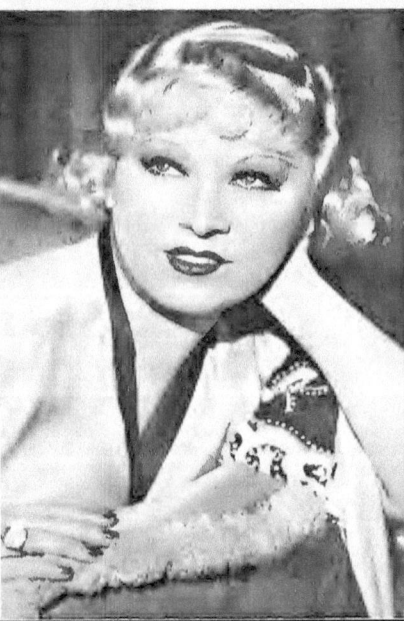

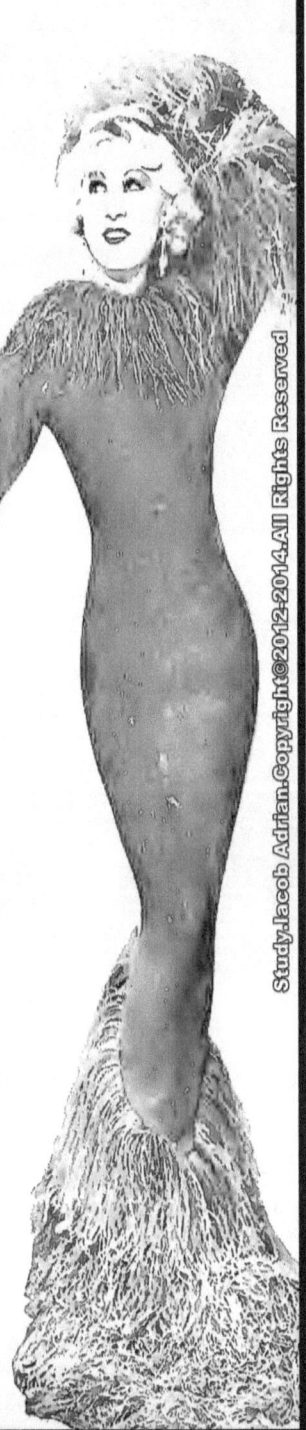

If Garbo Wears a Hat

The effect of Jean Harlow's platinum-blonde hair is well known. Many have attempted to emulate her. And, in days gone by, Colleen Moore's Dutch bob set a style for thousands of women and girls.

More recently, the "frou-frou" bangs assumed by Katharine Hepburn for her part of Jo in "Little Women" caught the fancy of the so-called "weaker sex" all over the world. To mention a single instance of their popularity, a hairdresser in a Kansas City beauty shop was obliged to cut out a picture of Miss Hepburn wearing the bangs and paste it on her mirror, so that she might study the full details, so many were the requests from her customers for that style of hair-dress.

Joan Crawford and Carole Lombard both have been important factors in setting new styles in hair, and each regularly receives a vast amount of fan mail from girls and women requesting advice on how to fix their tresses. Not infrequently stars are asked by beauty parlors to sponsor a new haircut, or some way of wearing the hair, and every smart shop religiously keeps up with the styles of coiffure as worn by the stars.

In furniture and house-furnishings, particularly, is seen the weight of the films. "Our Dancing Daughters," one of Joan Crawford's first successes, will be recalled as having introduced modernistic furniture to the American film public.

Later productions utilized this type of room decoration still more, and ere long the pulse of the furniture-buying populace was touched to the degree that thousands, and possibly millions, of homes now are furnished along modern lines. To Cedric Gibbons, head of the art department of Metro-Goldwyn and husband of Dolores Del Rio, goes the credit for the inception of this type of furniture on the screen.

Almost unbelievable are the number of requests from designers and manufacturers for new ideas in design. The point has been reached whereby a studio finds it nearly impossible to purchase furniture to dress any modern set, so marked is the influence of previous pictures on the pieces in the stores and in the factories. For this reason every studio has its own art department, which designs all modern furniture used in its productions.

Among recent pictures, "The Gay Divorcee" stands as an excellent example of a film play influencing the art decoration of the day. As you may recall, ultra-modern sets and furnishings featured every scene. The chromium fixtures especially intrigued the attention of the nation, and since the release of that hit, public and decorators alike have become "fixture-conscious." From all over this country and Europe, as well, there have been a large number of requests regarding new lighting effects.

Entire sets, too, prove a lure for the public to write to the studios. A wealthy surgeon of Boston, for instance, asked Paramount to send him a detailed plan of the Revolutionary-period living-room used in "Pursuit of Happiness," since he was building a summer home at Cape Cod and wished to construct his house about such a room.

A LARGE majority of the pieces played by orchestras were first heard on the screen. Particularly noteworthy is the fact that since "Stingaree"

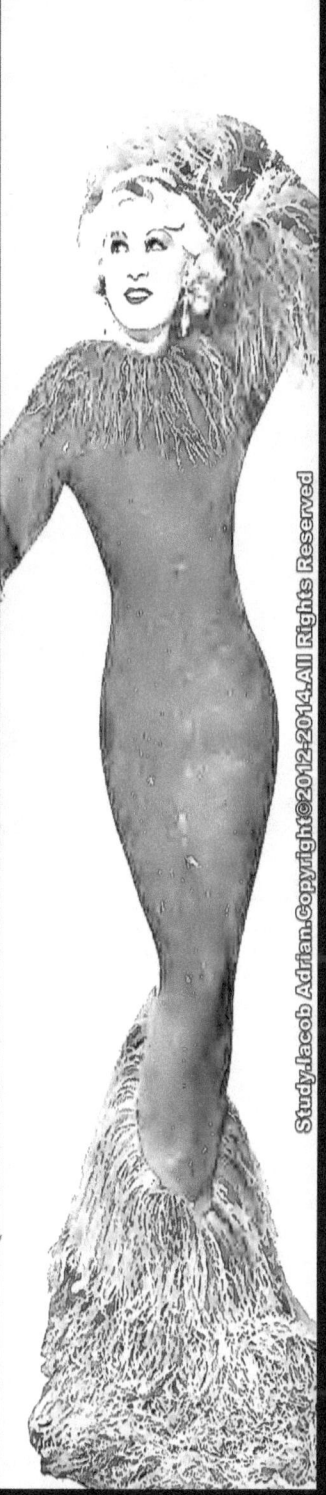

and "One Night of Love" the public has turned to grand opera in surprising numbers. Since those films reached the theaters, each with operatic scores, studios have been deluged with requests for more singing. "One Night of Love" in particular awakened for the first time the interest of many in grand opera. It produced a new appreciation of classical music.

Dancing, also, has been influenced largely by the films. Radio Pictures receive on an average 12,000 letters a month, asking how to dance the Carioca (seen in "Flying Down to Rio") and the Continental (from "The Gay Divorcee"). The national association of dancing teachers even has suggested that the studios ease up on their dances as presented on the screen . . . make them less difficult for the average couple.

When Edmund Lowe and Victor McLaglen directed their celebrated "Oh, yeah" bombardment upon one another, in their various pictures, they immediately popularized that expression, and Jack Oakie's "Skip it," in "From Hell to Heaven," likewise exercised its sway over the speech of the land. "Nuts," of course, has been heard in even the most conservative circles since "The Big Parade," some years ago.

WITH the age of sophistication on the screen manners have changed. Nearly every fan has some favorite after whom he patterns himself, either consciously or unconsciously, and many a one goes far out of his way in an attempt to be like his idol of the films.

By the same token, love-making has become more subtle, less a declamatory contest than formerly. Young swains, through having witnessed a picture lover woo his maid in a style which they admire, set out to win their lady-loves in much the same fashion.

Ronald Colman's reserve, Robert Montgomery's breeziness, Clark Gable's virility . . . all find their devotees among the young men of today. Gone are the days when the man bends his knee in proposal . . . the mode now is to sweep the girl off her feet. John Gilbert had a hand in this. Greater facility in speech and expression on these occasions may be credited to the potency of the screen.

In well-nigh every field, every branch of life, the movies exert influence. There can be little doubt but that the screen is one of the greatest forces for good, for advancement, known to present-day civilization . . . and Hollywood may well be proud of its effect upon the modes and manners of the day.

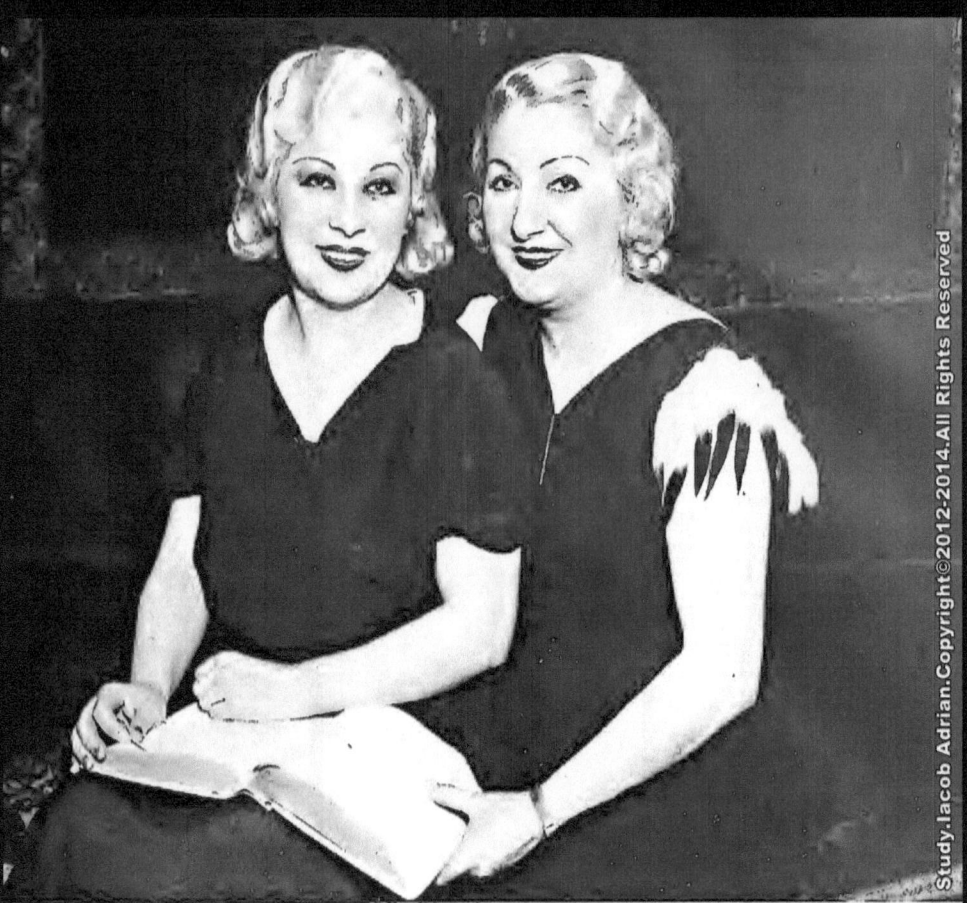

Mae West and her sister, Beverly, posing especially for The New Movie Magazine in their home.

BECAUSE . . .

Mae West Isn't

Diamond Lil

By HESTER ROBISON

IRONY of ironies! On the very site where Mae West was born there stands an imposing church. The grounds of her former Brooklyn, New York, homestead is the yard of a house of worship.

And, looking back beyond the days when Sex was Mae West's forte, one sees a chubby, flaxenhaired baby received as the favorite at church socials.

Surprise! Surprise! Down came our blinders for a better—and unique—look at Mae West as provided by her sister, Beverly, also an actress.

We went to see Beverly because we were told that she understood and loved her sister but saw her with unprejudiced eyes. Another reason we went to see Beverly, instead of going directly to Mae, was because we were wise to the exponent of sex in the theater and the movies; she likes you to think she is really tough. She wants you to believe she's part and parcel of the thing she represents as an actress—and it isn't so at all! You don't know the real girl!

THE first time we saw Mae was when she played in a lurid thing called "Sex," and the second time we saw her she was receiving the plaudits of a night club crowd in a gay place called "The Silver Slipper." The difference between the Mae West of the stage and the Mae West who bowed and smiled in the spotlight of a *hot-cha* place was about one yard of extra bustle in back and about two yards of extra bosom in front.

That was the first time we learned that Mae West, as theater audiences know her, is a fake. She's not tough and she's not fat and she's not vulgar. She puts it on and takes it off as she puts on and takes off the extra bust and bustle in her characterizations.

But knowing this was not enough preparation for the tale spun about Mae by her sister, Beverly. Knowing this hardly prepared us for the story of a home-town girl who made good in the big city, as related by Beverly. For the

The Real Story of the Real Girl Beneath the Curves,

Told for the First Time . . . . . and by Miss West's Sister

Because ... Mae West Isn't Diamond Lil

Because ...
Mae West Isn't
Diamond Lil

story of a girl who plays sexy roles without the refinement of Ruth Chatterton, who makes a bad woman bad when she plays a bad woman, yet who worshiped her mother to the day of her death, and who is clannish when it comes to her family.

BEVERLY, who looks very much like Mae, was more than eager to talk about her sister. "No one," she said wistfully, "seems to have bothered about Mae as she really is. They all write about how hard-boiled she is. They write about what they think must be her real life, based on what they know of her stage life. And they are far from the truth.

"Why don't they write about how Mae is up every morning at nine, working like a slave all day?

"Why don't they tell how she works until long past midnight studying her characters and writing plays and books with authentic backgrounds?"

We suggested that maybe it was because no one had troubled to tell the public about Mae—and that started Beverly off on her favorite topic, her sister.

"A lot of people censure Mae for wearing the extreme clothes she does," said Beverly, settling herself cozily into a huge chair. "The idea of wearing extreme clothes was mother's. She was French and had worked as a stylist, so she naturally believed in dressing originally. Mae was always voluptuous looking, even as a little girl, so mother told her to wear clothes that showed off her figure. Long before European styles became fashionable over here, mother bought Paris clothes for Mae."

Beverly, pausing to reflect on the matter of clothes, began to laugh. "It's strange," she said, "what ideas clothes will give people. The fact that Mae wore extreme fashions gave them the idea that she was fast. I suppose mother knew this and that's why she kept an eagle eye on Mae all the time. She didn't have to, though, for Mae's whole life centered about mother and mother's wishes.

"About three years ago mother died." Beverly closed her eyes as if to exclude the idea from her conscious self. "If those who think Mae is hardboiled could have seen her then, they would have changed their minds. She forgot all about her career. She dropped all of her plans for tours throughout the country and came rushing back to New York to be with mother. That's a side of Mae that no one outside of the family has seen. It's a side she keeps jealously hidden from the public. She doesn't believe in disillusioning them."

AS Beverly talked we had flashes of Mae as the public knows her. Mae saying "Hello, kid, been insulted lately?" And Mae whisking sexily through a room or stopping to put heat into a love scene.

"Mae," her sister said, "started being a professional when she was twelve. She never did care to play with other children; they seemed silly to her. By the time she was twelve Mae was playing in a stock company. She had studied dramatics but what she preferred was singing and dancing. And"— she was very emphatic— "even as a little girl Mae's character songs were risqué. She knew she looked voluptuous and she knew that she should do something in keeping with her appearance. Mother realized that a career was one thing, private life another, so she agreed with Mae.

"You hear about so many girls having been discovered by Ziegfeld," Beverly said with a gentle hint of sarcasm. "Mae was really discovered by him. He liked her appearance and her frank way of singing sexy songs and the way she danced, so he featured her in the Folies Bergère. Mother used to meet her backstage and take her home. In those days Mae had a tutor because she didn't have time to go to school.

"After Ziegfeld, she played at Hammerstein's theater on Broadway and Forty-second Street. She knew her stuff was good when Hammerstein held her over for six weeks—quite a success in those days."

THE telephone rang and Beverly got up to answer it. She came back grinning. "Someone wants Mae to look at a play he's written. Everyone in the theater knows she's a softy when it comes to helping. Mae thinks she's gotten along because she's helped others; they've gotten famous and in turn have helped her. It's a circle, see? And she's smart enough to know it."

Ever since the days when she helped a certain young man to fame, Mae has been known in the theater as a picker of winners. The story, as Beverly told it, is a study in human interest:

"Years ago when Mae was touring in vaudeville she needed a pianist to fill out her act," Beverly said. "She let the fact be known—things are done that way in the theater—not by advertising. Someone sent a good-looking young man up to see her. He could certainly play the piano. When he sat down that piano fairly sang. And he had a certain charm about him, too. Mae took a liking to him."

"One day," Beverly said, "he and Mae were talking and he started to sing a little. Then he blushed and looked up and stopped singing suddenly. He said he didn't like to sing because he had a slight lisp and he was afraid people would laugh at him. Mae didn't laugh. She'd liked the sample of his voice and she urged him to sing a few numbers. After he finished Mae looked him straight in the eyes and she told him he should be ashamed to keep that voice a secret. And she said his lisp was fascinating.

"'It won't be long,' Mae told him, 'when women will fall for that lisp and crave to hear it.'"

MAE WEST was a truthful prophet, for shortly afterwards the young man was snatched up by a Broadway producer and today he is one of the highest paid singers on the stage or on radio. His name is—Harry Richman.

"Why is it," we asked, "that Mae has never married?"

"I suppose," said sister Beverly, "you could say that Mae was selfish about her career. She believes you can't be a successful actress and have your mind and heart on something else. Marriage would take too much of her away from her work. She doesn't even like to devote herself to a romance because it interferes with her work. You must remember," cautioned Beverly, "that Mae isn't just an actress. She's a playwright, she produces and directs her own shows and looks after every little detail.

"When she produced 'Diamond Lil' David Belasco came backstage and congratulated her on the authenticity of everything in the play," said Beverly. "You don't suppose it's authentic because Mae is that type of woman herself, do you?

"She doesn't care for night clubs," said Beverly. "Mae never did go much for night life. And—believe it or not—most people think it's a fairy story—Mae doesn't drink or smoke. She guards her health; and her voice is husky enough without making it harsh from stimulants. I've had people tell me she's putting on an act about not drinking, but it's really true.

"I don't want you to get the idea," Beverly warned, "that Mae is a self-sacrificing home-girl who looks longingly at the kitchen stove and yearns to hear the kettle sing. She wouldn't cook if she had to and she despises housework of any kind. . . ."

A KEY was fitted into the latch and we heard sounds of someone blustering in. We looked up and there stood Mae, blonde and white and pink and shockingly small. She weighs only 118 pounds and seems one-third the size of her stage and screen self. Her neck is somewhat thick for her size and that gives her an appearance of stoutness which she does not actually have. Yet, small as she is, she seems the personification of physical appeal. One can see how, with the addition of a fake bust and bustle, she can be transformed into a seducer of men of thirty or more years ago.

Mae sat down on a divan and curled her legs under her.

"Do you think I'm bad?" she asked.

"People have come right up to me and said I couldn't play bad women without being bad myself or knowing and liking that kind of women. I'm going to be honest with you now! In all my life I've never met a really bad woman—and the reason I can make them so glamorous on the stage is because they're not real."

IT was a truism with which we could not argue. Mae West herself is not glamorous. Greta Garbo, Katharine Hepburn, Ruth Chatterton, Kay Francis—name any of the screen's exponents of glamour—they're not glamorous off-screen or offstage. They are all, as Beverly West put it, "nice girls who made good by hard work—and there isn't any glamour in hard work."

THE BOULEVARDIER ELECTS

Queen Mae

MISS MAE WEST barges into our Hall of Fame this month as majestic as a Ptolemy and takes her place on the throne beside King Cagney. Match that for a royal pair! Queen Mae says Jimmy is the only one in Hollywood that's got anything like her style. "Animal personality," Mae says. "Gives them the rough stuff right out like I do."

How'd you like to see them as "Antony and Cleopatra" up to date? Write your congressman.

Note to Her Majesty:

DEAR QUEEN: I feel I owe you an explanation. In my Hall of Fame a couple of months back I tried to make it plain you were my Dream Girl (Ten years ago it was Lillian Gish. How dreams change!)

On page 94 of my little masterpiece I said right out, "Mae West is my Dream Girl," adding Connie Cummings and Heppy Hepburn as substitutes in case you went to jail or somewhere. . . . . You know, like in the picture. But the editor apparently was in one of his holiday moods when he put the story together, for on the first page he crates a dozen sunkist babies and labels them My Dream Girls. Nice girls. I didn't mind. But I can imagine how you felt, a stranger in Hollywood not knowing who to trust. Probably thought I was giving you the run around. Nothing like that, Queen.

When I composed that Hall of Fame I hadn't seen "She Done Him Wrong," so if I felt like that then you can imagine how I feel now. Wonder Woman.

I sat through two shows of "She Done Him Wrong" and when the doors opened the next morning there stood the Boulevardier, twirling his mustaches, with a neatly packed lunch. I thought it greater than "Cavalcade." I mean to a rugged American the Bowery means more than the Boer War, naturally.

Seriously, Miss West, you gave a performance far finer than some the old doodle bugs of the Motion Picture Academy hand out those statues and speeches for. But we won't go into that racket now.

You have brought to the screen a new method and timing, to say nothing of that gorgeous animal personality. I like your motto: "Never embarrass the audience. Stifle the blush with a laugh." That's the way with men too, and how you know your men, Mae! Reminding us how women used to look before they put on pants as a master stroke. I haven't seen so much beauty bulging out of a gown since I wooed Lillian Russell (I was known as Diamond Jim Brady then).

(Please turn to page 97)

New Movie Magazine's strolling scribbler—as personified by HERB HOWE—puts her on the throne beside King Cagney

How'd you like to see them as "Antony and Cleopatra" up to date? Write your congressman about it.

Queen Mae

I'd like to do a story with you, Mae, for the July issue. That being the hottest month I figured it sort of appropriate. Anyhow I'll be around to have my fortune told. Until then—

Tout a vous—H. H.

P. S. They tell me that twenty-five pounds of you in that picture was pads. How about autographing a pound for a pal?

OH, Mae. I can't help advising you. Must be the paternal in me or something. For Gossakes, Mae, don't turn on us now and become a Hollywood Lady. Don't go dramatic. Or demand Sympathy. Or talk about your friends among the Royalty. Give us a New Deal like Mr. Roosevelt. We're so oppressed with dukes and countesses and bawths and sicrtries and artistes striving for Higher Things. And sophisticates who talk like fallen ladies are supposed to but don't. Say nothing of Garbo imitations. Actually, Mae, you are the first gal arriving in Hollywood in a long time who hasn't tried to copy Greta. For that reason you are most like her essentially. I mean, you are yourself. And *now* will you tell my fortune?

Latest Arrivals in The Hall of Fame.
Miss Diana Wynyard from "Cavalcade."

Mr. Buster Crabbe, King of the Jungle, accompanied by Jackie the Lion.

Miss Ruth Donnelly after handling "Hard to Handle" Cagney.

Mr. Franchot Tone, arriving the day after "Today We Live."

Miss Ruby Keeler from "42nd Street."

Master Leroy Winebrunner, 8 months' old picture bandit, after taking Chevalier for a ride in "A Bedtime Story."

Mr. Brian Aherne, leading man with Katharine Cornell, will probably arrive in the gallery of the great with "The Song of Songs." If he proves as lyrical as his name he should achieve romantic heights. It easily takes the prize for euphony, pronounced with the Irish cadence: Bree-AHN Ah-HERN.

(*Please turn to page 98*)

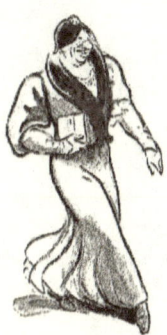

With Paramount grabbing all that publicity for Marlene's pants, I suggested at M-G-M that Wally Beery be trotted out in one of Adrian's cute little frocks.

Queen Mae

MISS DIANA WYNYARD has already joined the company of Hollywood's Immortals. She has been footprinted in the forecourt of Grauman's Chinese theater. The ceremony attending the pedal impression was marked by a hands-across-the-sea feeling—England's "God Save The King," Hollywood's "Let's Put Out The Lights," and a stirring eulogy of Miss Wynyard's genius by Mr. Sid Grauman, at the conclusion of which he inquired her name, having failed to make a note of that.

While Miss Wynyard was solemnly sinking into the wet cement I ambled about under the cocos plumosas and the jasper-hued canopies making notes of the famous feet that had preceded hers. There were Mary Pickford's, of course. And not far away a block imprinted by Marie Dressler and Wally Beery and scrawled, rather unfortunately it seemed to me, "America's New Sweethearts." Jackie Cooper's block had a mortuary aspect with the inscription, "Jackie Cooper, America's Boy, Age 8 years." Beside Gloria Swanson's sharply indented heels was a pierced heart and the words "Always to Sid." There were tracks of many other great artists, including those of Tony, Tom Mix's horse. Medi-

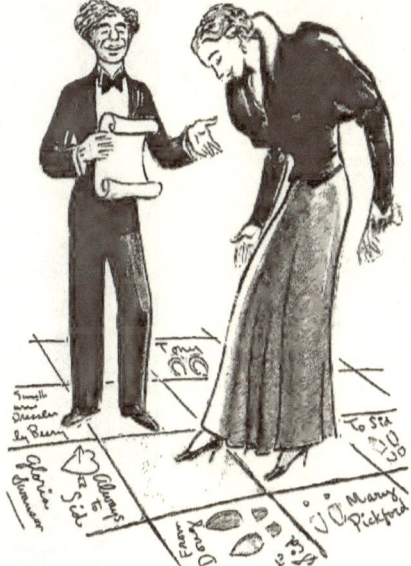

And now Diana Wynyard has put her foot down in the Movie Hall of Fame.

tating on the evanescence of screen fame I found solace in the thought that here in this solid concrete their names would be preserved forever for posterity. That is, I did until told that the blocks were removable and would be taken up when their box office receipts fell off.

ONE line from "Cavalcade" keeps rippling oddly through my memory. Perhaps it was the beauty of the childish inflection. It was spoken by the little boy on the balcony as he observed Queen Victoria's bier: "She must have been a very little lady, Mother."

Incidentally, I have never heard English spoken more beautifully than by those children.

"CAVALCADE" has a special value for us Americans in defining more clearly those precious traits of English character: dignity, courage, justice, loyalty. For the first time, I think, I felt a twinge of filial affection for Mother England.

Before I go further I'd better announce that the Come-On Inn over whose passing I whimpered so pathetically a couple of months ago did not pass out after all. It was saved from the brink, I gather, by the opportune return of Malcolm McGregor. The following tart note offering me choice of pistols or potato mashers came from Betty, the chatelaine, who trundles the trays while Hattie, my true love, stuffs peppers in the kitchen.

"What do you mean by saying the Come-On Inn has closed up? It is wide open and doing nicely." (Permit me to interpose at this point that by wide open she doesn't mean wet) "So you better correct it in the next number of the NEW MOVIE. Maybe you think because you haven't been in here for some time we had to close but Malcolm McGregor is back in pictures so you can see we fooled you because we still have him. . . . Love and Kisses—Betty."

Dear Betty:
I am glad to hear that Mal is enjoying such a good appetite. I hope he will keep the Come-On Inn thriving for many years, just as I did until the soup kitchens opened. Wistfully—Herb.

EVERY lot has its pet. Clark Gable is the sweetheart of M-G-M. He's as popular off screen with the boys as he is on with the girls. For that matter, no one has heard the girlies screaming at his approach in the flesh.

YESTERDAY four publicity whip-poorwills surrounded me in Howard Strickling's office and started twittering on the theme of What-An-Athlete Gable. Seems he started shooting golf at 118 and in less than three months was shooting 84. Learned to ride a year ago and now goes over precipices like the Italian cavalry. Tennis—boy! if he wasn't such a gentleman he'd show Helen Wills. He lunches and pals with props, electricians and even press agents, not because he's trying to be democratic but because he would improve. You can't learn anything lunching with actors, Lord knows. He detests premieres and only attends to oblige the publicity boys. Two of them have to steer him through the crowds, otherwise he'd get lost signing autographs. He's got a grin like the sun o'er the Sierras. Starts calling you by your nickname before you know he knows it and, in all in all, has the friendly approach that would make him a whale of a panhandler.

I DROVE down on the back lot to see ol' pal Gable do his stuff in "The White Sister." You need a car to get around the M-G-M acreage. I drove through a street lined with breweries, respectfully removing my hat as I did so—where Jimmy Durante made "What—No Beer?"—and on past a railroad station with real pullman coaches on real tracks that connect by outside switches with the P. E. main line—so real they catch actors trying to bum rides back to New York.

I saw Clark's brown Packard roadster in front of a very old Italian convent which is the very last place you'd expect to find Mr. Gable's car. Entering the gate I passed through a quiet courtyard blooming with flowers that looked so natural I couldn't believe they were paper even after pinching them. Clark was in Italian uniform, which makes any man handsome so you can guess what it does to him.

"Hello!" he called with that ingratiating air that will mint dimes if he ever has to make touches.

"The boys have been telling me what a great athlete you are," I said when he ambled over.

"Hope you haven't come to make me prove it."

"No. Just wanted to see if by any chance you were an actor, too."

"No," he echoed beaming. "Can prove that in a minute."

WITH Paramount grabbing all that publicity for Marlene's pants I suggested at M-G-M that Wally Beery be trotted forth in one of Adrian's little frocks. The objection to that was it would just be augmenting the Dietrich publicity. On the contrary, I argued, it would be kidding the pants off Marlene. Surely a worth while achievement. And that's what it did. Wheeler and Woolsey flounced skirtishly into the Brown Derby for lunch, and that evening Marlene was seen dancing at the Cocoanut Grove with her skirt on (fooled us).

When Cary Grant refused a cigarette, saying he didn't smoke, Mae West retorted: "Smoking is going to make a man look effeminate before long." So's wearing pants. I don't know how a man will assert his sex. About the only way is for him to dress like Tarzan. Then if the girls copy . . . Well!

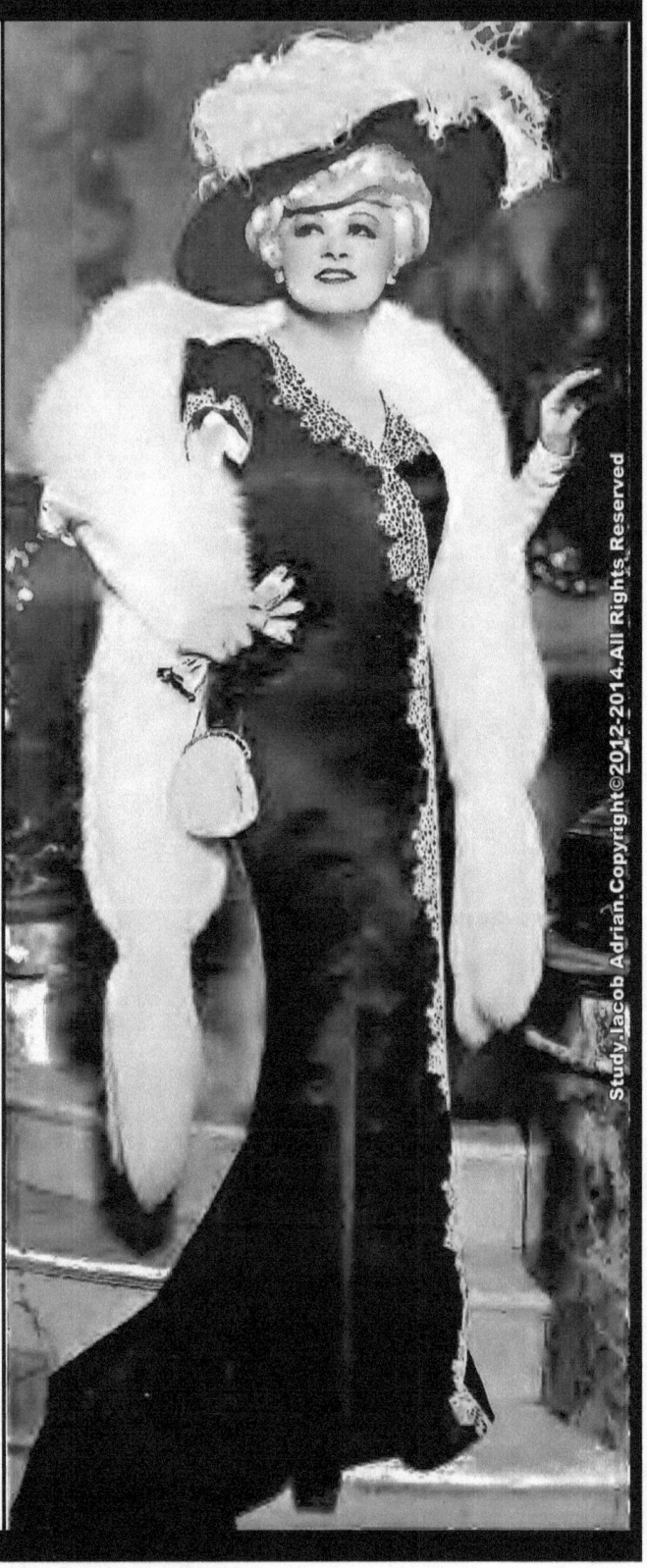

Ted Cook's

MOVIE COOK-COOS

"PROBABLY the sort of thing that I present on the screen is just what the folks need these days," says Mae West.

Anyway, it's probably the sort of thing a lot of gals could use these days.

A RING, valued at $5,000, which Carole Lombard reported lost, was returned to the actress after being discovered in a gutter near the front of Paramount studios.

Found, no doubt, by a scenario writer poking around for ideas.

> Gals who pose and hide their legs
> Are thought less of by many eggs.

Most heart-rending news story of the month:

"Ruby Keeler was so upset by the earthquake that she could neither eat nor sleep. In order to quiet her, Al Jolson, her husband, went out and bought her a beautiful diamond and jade brooch, shaped like a basket of fruit."

Some enterprising Hollywood druggist will likely make a fortune from this newly discovered insomnia cure. He'll put up diamond and jade brooches in bottles.

Miss Keeler got her brooch as a result of an earthquake. Most movie girls get their brooches by just threatening an earthquake.

> No matter what dire poverty
> The heroine of shifty shows,
> She always can afford, we see,
> The most expensive underclothes.

JEAN HARLOW says:
"The only time I ever forget myself, really, is when I am hammering at my typewriter."

Which just goes to show that Jean is different.

Most blondes are apt to forget themselves when they aren't typewriting.

> And also it's hard to have attitudes pliant
> Toward photos of female stars looking defiant.

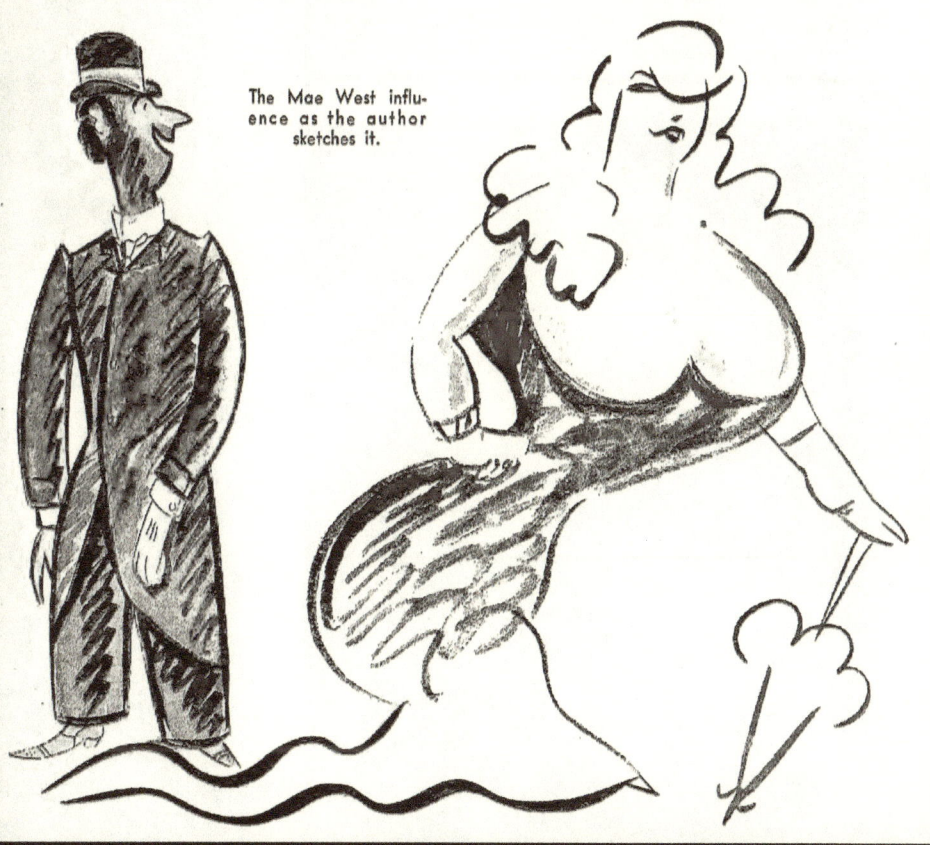

The Mae West influence as the author sketches it.

Movie Cook-Coos

Add similies—
Suggestive as a supervisor.

And in Hollywood, right now, it's just like a woman not to be.

OMIGOSH!
(Classified Ad—Los Angeles paper)

BABIES! BABIES! BABIES! Brought to attention of motion picture directors at once. Box T-174.

When a film star's life is an open book
No chatter writer cares to look.

AND right at present, it seems there are two schools of thought on the subject of what's wrong with the motion picture industry. One faction thinks it needs a dictator, while the rest of us think it needs big shots who are willing to listen.

What if it all started just because Marlene Dietrich's husband bought a two-pants suit?

LET them make more and worse pictures—and then charge the actors a tidy sum to keep them out of circulation.

Will Hays might even induce the Red Cross to step in with contributions to ease human suffering.

In not a movie has there been
A gal who walked with hands on hips
Who didn't prove quite steeped in sin
And guilty of a lot of slips.

Be that as it may, Hollywood

has certainly speeded up production of things something must be done about.

Would any of you kiddies out there in magazine-land be interested in the fact that Jean Harlow has double-jointed thumbs?
No?
All right! All right for you!
We'll just save the handsome silver loving-cup for another occasion.

AND it seems there are a lot of producers who can't decide whether to treat sex as a necessary evil or to treat sex as a very necessary evil.

PEGGY Hopkins Joyce announces that she is planning to go big game hunting in Africa.
Heretofore Peggy has done her big game hunting in Chicago, New York, Paris and Hollywood.

(She ought to have Jack Oakie stuffed and placed in her trophy room.)

"I have another idea* in the back of my head," says Peggy. "I want to write a novel. My publisher says it ought to be about Hollywood. I think Hollywood is too tame. Perhaps, however, I'll capitulate."

Well, why not?

A modern novelist has got to get material somehow.

The late beloved Wilson Mizner once warned that in Hollywood, two ideas at the same time are considered unlawful assemblage.

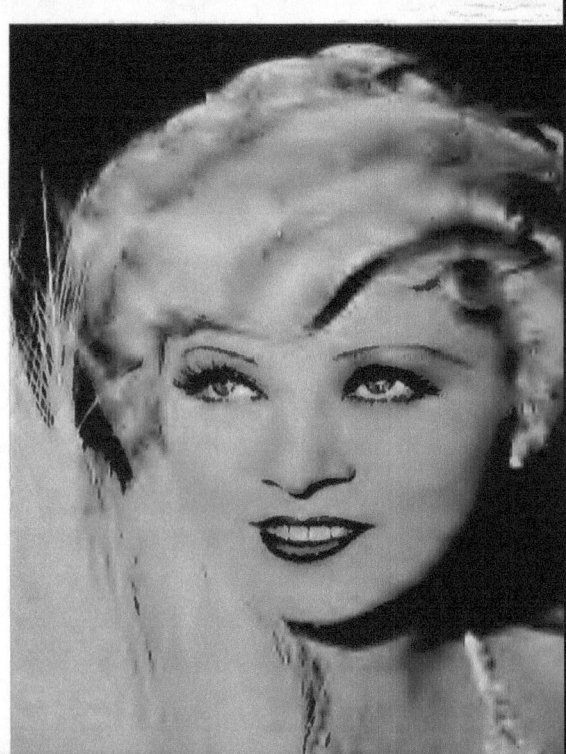

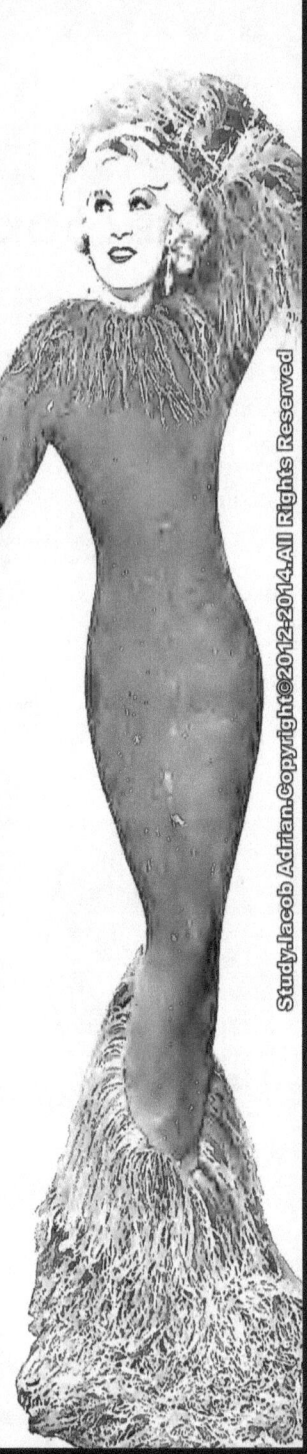

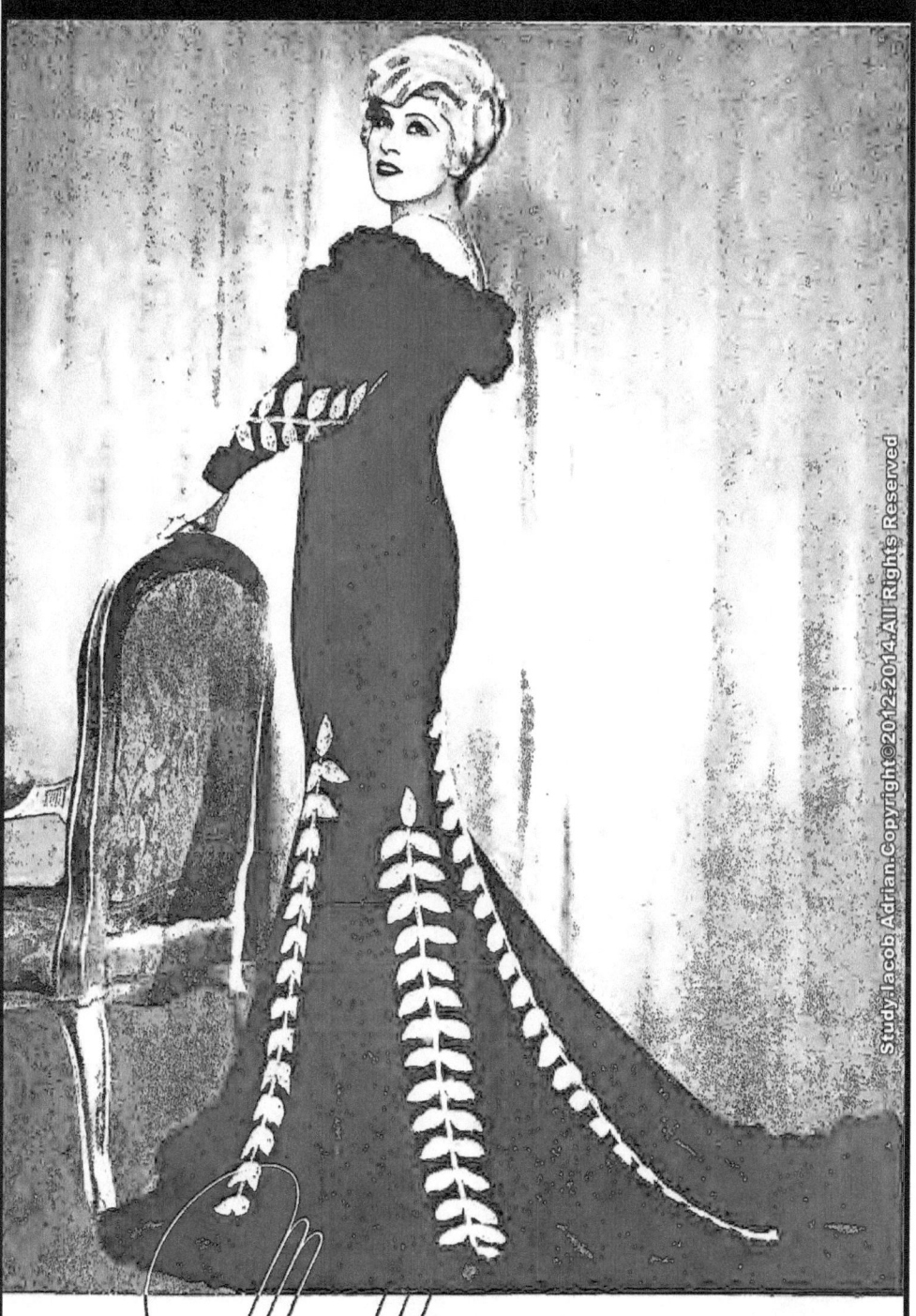

Mae West in "IT AIN'T NO SIN"

with Roger Pryor, John Mack Brown. Duke Ellington & Band...Directed by Leo McCarey
if it's a PARAMOUNT PICTURE...it's the best show in town!

How much MONEY

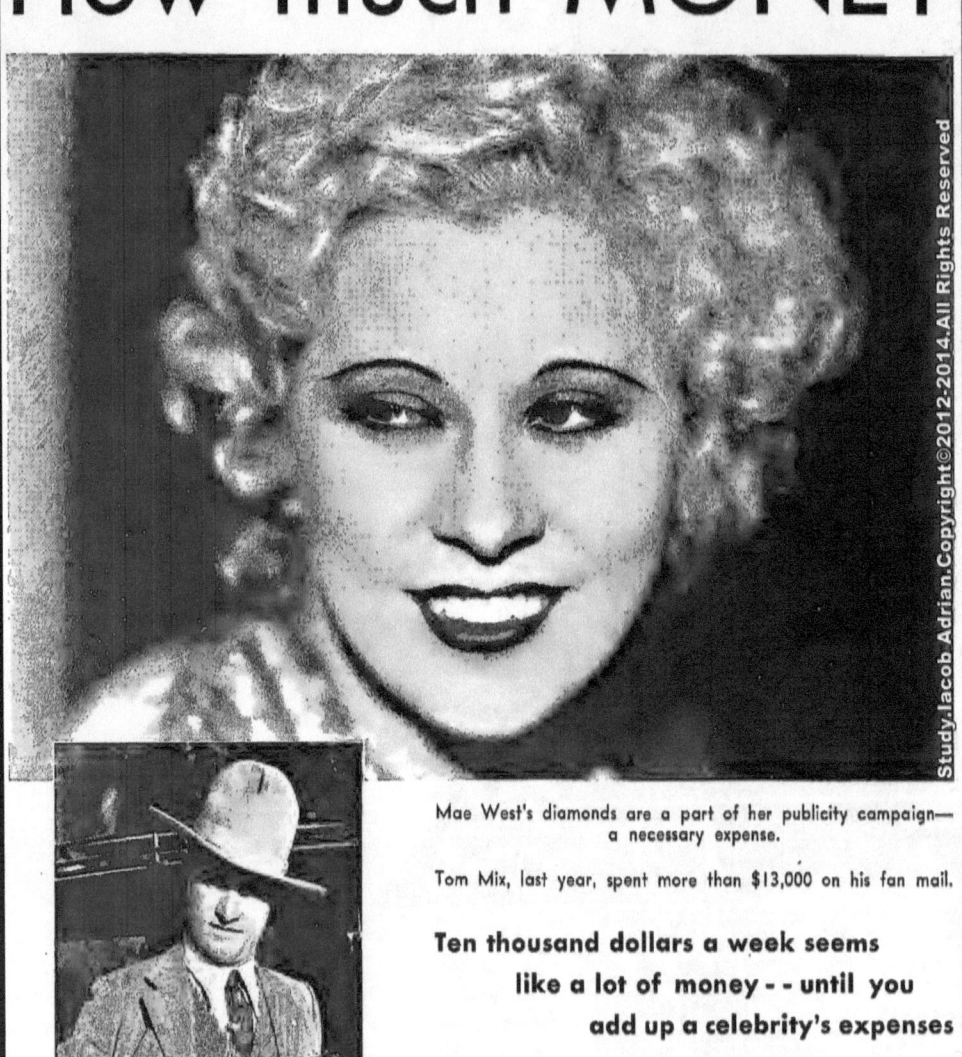

Mae West's diamonds are a part of her publicity campaign—a necessary expense.

Tom Mix, last year, spent more than $13,000 on his fan mail.

Ten thousand dollars a week seems like a lot of money - - until you add up a celebrity's expenses

HOLLYWOOD is a gold mine. Its stars supply the gold—and the rest of the world supplies the miners. And how those miners *dig!*

Lured by tales—and only too true they are—of the prodigal extravagances of Movietown's *nouveau riche*, an army of money-at-any-price huntsmen has declared open season on John and Jane Star's pocketbooks, and canny indeed is the film celebrity who salvages twenty per cent. of his pay check.

Looting the stars is not a new pursuit, and the looters have always been cunning. But now, with their wits sharpened by the depression, they are like a pack of famished arctic wolves.

With "chiselers" to the left of him, racketeers to the right of him, blackmailers just ahead of him—and his own lavish follies leading him ever deeper into the morass of financial distress . . .

What chance has a motion-picture star to save his money?

Remember—he is forced to meet hundreds of "necessary" expenses that are unknown to the average man of equal

does a Star have left?

By **ERIC L. ERGENBRIGHT** who investigated the great "Hollywood Swindle" for The New Movie Magazine

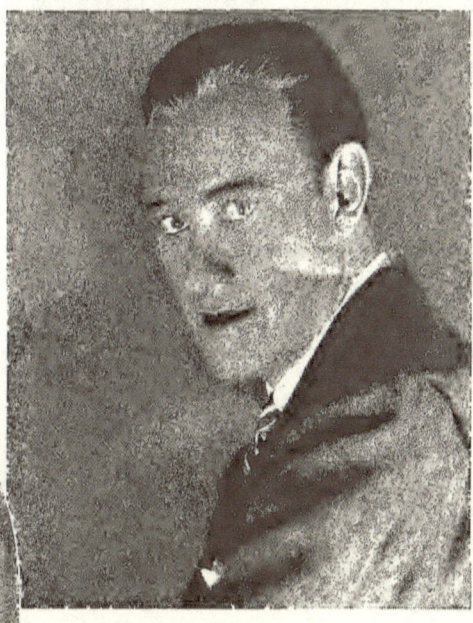

Conrad Nagel, head of the Motion Picture Relief Fund, estimates that more than $2,000,000 a year goes out of Hollywood to "fake charities."

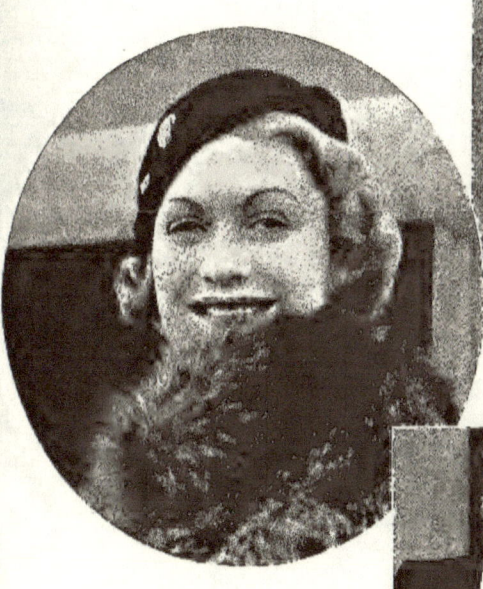

Constance Bennett spent $12,000 during the past year on stamps, stationery and professional photographs.

Wallace Beery fought a girl's attempt to sue him, ran a barrage of publicity, spent a small fortune, but won.

income. He must be—or, at least, thinks he must be—eternally surrounded by high-priced agents, managers, attorneys, publicity men, secretaries, servants and bodyguards.

Being in the public eye, he believes that he must "put up a front."

Temperamentally, he is made to order for the schemes of the blackmailer, for he recalls how many stars have faded in the withering glare of adverse publicity. He knows that Mr. and Mrs. Public are cruelly eager to believe the worst of their idols; consequently he lives in terror of scandal.

In another particular he is the ready prey of petty larceny racketeers—he is by nature over-emotional, too quick to sympathize. A sob story, well told, sends his hand flying to his bill-fold.

B^{UT} let's leave the blackmailer, the panhandler, the racketeer and their ilk for more specific mention later, and consider, first of all, the star's "necessary" expenses.

It is, of course, impossible to list the expenditures of one star and truthfully represent them as the exact expenses of every other star. It is also impossible to draw definite lines between legitimate expenses, idiotic extravagance and tribute to the various classes and degrees of swindlers.

Our "star" then, is not an individual but a composite representing the group to which he belongs. He has been created only after scanning the expense sheets of several stars. We'll assume that he's married, has one child, is paying alimony to one ex-wife and that he receives one of those ten thousand-a-week salaries which excite the envy and sometimes the indignation of the rest of us.

How much of his salary can he call his own?

In the first place, his contract with the studio calls for forty weeks a year, not for fifty-two. Therefore, his weekly wage, spread over the entire year, is $7,692.30—*not* $10,000.

His agent is not far from the cashier's window on pay day. He takes a neat ten per cent. of our star's wages. Perhaps he landed the contract for him two years ago, and has done

How Much Money?

nothing but play golf ever since—but that makes no difference. An agent's percentage—almost invariably ten per cent.—endures for the life of the contract and sometimes a good deal longer. Our star now has $6,923 to show for his week's toil.

Uncle Sam, sternest of creditors, is next in line. He nicks our star for approximately forty-eight per cent. of the $6,923, and leaves him staring a bit ruefully at the $3,601 remaining in his possession.

As long as we've started keeping books "by the week," let's continue on that basis, dividing monthly expenses by four and annual outlays, such as insurance and taxes, by fifty-two. The line forms to the right, and our star pays until it hurts—knowing, as he does so, that a tidy portion of his lucre is going to the Hollywood swindle and that many of his bills are padded out of all proportion. Let's check off the items.

First, there's the hired help

Attorney (paid an annual retainer fee)	$ 65.00
Publicity Counsel (who has other clients, of course	65.00
Secretary (Real intelligence is needed here)	75.00
Chauffeur (Many stars employ two of them)	50.00
Cook (We stars call him a chef and pay accordingly)	60.00
Housekeeper (We list her and get along without a butler)	50.00
Mrs. Star's personal maid	40.00
Personal valet (a studio necessity)	40.00
Second Maid	30.00
Gardener (He probably has two, but we'll trim a bit)	35.00
Trainer (Our star loses his contract if he gets paunchy)	40.00
Bodyguard (Dietrich employs two, others even more)	40.00
Governess for Junior	50.00
	———
Total	$640.00

WE'VE been very conservative, but our star has only $2,961—and he isn't through paying, not by any means. He's just hitting his stride. Look!

House Rent (he has comparatively simple taste, too)	$ 240.00
Beach House Rental (four months' rental spread over a period of fifty-two weeks)	62.50
Groceries (remember that retinue of servants.)	150.00
Clothing (there's Mrs. Star and Junior to buy for)	240.00
Alimony (and if Johnny gets off this easy, he's lucky)	200.00
Fan Mail Expense (stationery, stamps, photos and steno)	225.00
Clipping Bureau Service (one must check his publicity)	15.00
Publicity Lunches (an interviewer never pays his own check)	5.00

Personal Photographs (art photography comes high)	$ 25.00
Advertising in trade journals	30.00
Automobile Expense (depreciation, upkeep, insurance and so forth on two first-class cars)	75.00
Dentist	15.00
Doctor	30.00
Pocket Money (for both Mr. and Mrs. Star)	150.00
Entertainment (and our star doesn't go in for big parties)	50.00
Total	$1,532.50

HE looks at the $1,428.50 which is still on hand, recalls that host of annoying little expenses, like barber shop and beauty parlor bills, ice cream cones, toothpaste, make-up, radio tubes, chewing gum, cigars, golf balls, etc.—and gives orders to balance the budget, darn it!

But wait! How about that $500,000 life insurance policy, taken out when you're thirty, Mr. Star? True, it's an investment, but you can't collect on it now and the premiums amount to $295 a week. And that $25,000 policy on the missus will cost you another ten dollars.

And listen, old timer, if you will own personal property—furs, jewels, paintings, furniture, automobiles, etc.—assessed at $100,000, you must pay the county taxes at the rate of $79 a week. And how about your club dues, and—oh, gosh!—that bill your bootlegger's been trying to collect? The Community Chest expects a heavy contribution from you, and you can't be niggardly—not in your position! And Motion Picture Relief fund demands one-half of one per cent. of your salary. And you can't forget all those distant relatives you've been supporting—people would *talk* if you did.

With a sigh, Johnny deducts $100 for the Community Chest, $38.46 for the Relief Fund, $200 for the relatives and needy friends and sets aside another $50 for the various emergency charities which will ask his support during the week.

The princely sum with which he started is now whittled down to about $500—and *you* and *you* and *you* are calling him a "sap," an extravagant fool.

Perhaps he is, but he is also the victim of systematic looting.

FOR instance, some merchants may deliberately mark up their prices when an "in-the-money" star enters their doors.

One woman star—who pays dearly for her "best-dressed women" title—told me of her recent experience in buying a scarf. The shop was crowded. While she waited for service, she inspected a number of openly displayed scarfs. The one she wanted carried a six-dollar price tag. Finally, a clerk waited on her, and, when asked to show that particular scarf, deftly hid the tag and informed her that it was priced at nine dollars!

Dick Arlen tells of his experiences with a grocer. His monthly bills had been averaging $260—and Dick and Joby live very simply. Convinced that

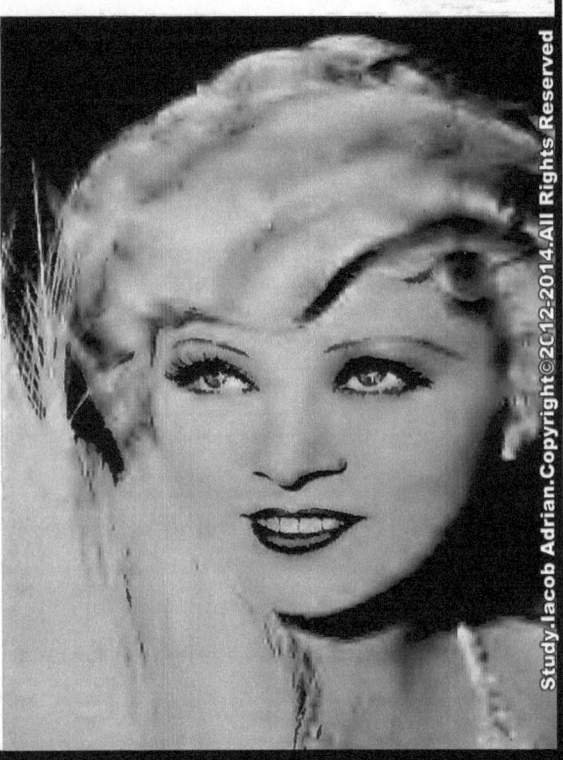

How Much Money?

How Much Money?

he was being overcharged, Arlen instructed his secretary to buy anonymously. During the following month, the bill dropped to $73.

These are not isolated cases, but everyday examples of a wide-spread practice which robs Hollywood's stars of untold thousands every month.

I talked to Rex Cole, president of the Equitable Investment Corporation, and manager of the financial affairs of at least a score of famous stars.

"My clients," he said, "report one padded bill after another. To my certain knowledge, stars are often charged double the price paid by non-professional customers.

"Not only unscrupulous merchants, but a number of dentists, doctors and other professional men make a practice of overcharging high-salaried players. For example, a certain client of mine who is a well-known actress, recently underwent an operation. She did not bargain in advance with the surgeon, for she knew that the customary charge for that particular operation is $500.

"She received a bill for $5,000! When she brought it to me I called on the doctor and filed an indignant protest. He shrugged, said, 'She can afford to pay,' and threatened to sue. Ultimately, my client settled for $3,500.

"A great many dishonest servants have helped merchants rob their employers in return for a commission on the star's purchases. A few merchants have also racketeered by sending unordered merchandise to the star's home, obtaining the signature of an unsuspecting servant and then submitting a bill."

REX COLE knows whereof he speaks —and, for that matter, didn't *I*, just a few weeks ago, hear a dentist tell about charging one of our most noted screen lovers $1,000 for a simple extraction? I did. Moreover, I know that that same dentist charges his average patient exactly ten dollars for an identical extraction.

He explained the $990 by stating that the star is a heavy drinker, that he insisted on taking gas, and that, had he died of heart failure while in the chair, the resultant newspaper furore would have ruined any dentist's practice.

And didn't the ultra-conservative Conrad Nagel amaze me with the nerve-racking experience of one of his best friends, a certain noted director? It seems that the director authorized his housekeeper, in whom he had every confidence, to act as purchasing agent for the family. She promptly abused the trust by buying thousands of dollars' worth of merchandise on her employer's accounts. Presumably, she resold the goods—at least, the director was never aware of their purchase. She also destroyed the merchants' statements.

The director was a man who prided himself on being "good pay." Yet he became known as a "dead beat." One night, at a Chamber of Commerce meeting, he was openly hissed. He was bewildered and hurt. Finally a friend explained the merchants' attitude—and the whole affair was revealed.

Perhaps you begin to realize why our star can't save money. Even when he insures his personal property against fire and theft, he must pay exactly double the premium charged you and me. We pay one and one-quarter per cent.; an actor must pay two and one-half per cent.

Many insurance companies now refuse to issue public liability policies to our star, who must, therefore, drive his Rolls at his own risk. The refusal is based on the fact that the star, because of his fame and much-publicized income, is sued for damages every time he brushes someone's fender.

And not only is he sued for much more than he would be if he were an average citizen, but the jury, being envious of his salary, awards the plaintiff plenty, whether he has actually been damaged or not.

Lawsuits are the bane of a star's existence. It's a rare day which does not witness a new assault, via the courts, on some film notable's purse. Stars have found it cheaper to employ an attorney by the year than by the case. Frequently the suits brought against stars have no foundation in fact. Therefore, the lawyer who urges the plaintiff on shrewdly hopes that the case will be settled out of court. And records prove that his hopes materialize about seven times out of ten. The star knows that it costs much money and even more inconvenience to fight even the most unjust damage suit. Furthermore, he *dreads adverse publicity.*

IN that dread lies the blackmailer's strangle-hold on Hollywood. Blackmail has swept the movie colony like a plague. So prevalent has it become that the district attorney, Buron Fitts, recently established a special department to fight the menace. Already his officers have investigated 250 cases involving stars, directors and producers, yet . . .

"Not more than one-tenth of the

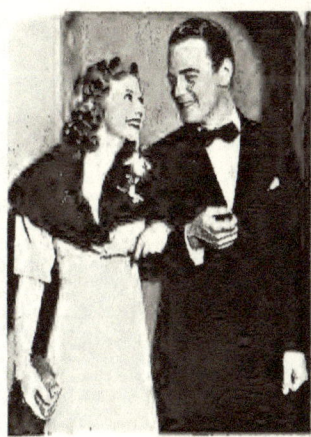

Ginger Rogers was the first girl to step out publicly with Lew Ayres after his divorce. Whereupon both had to deny to a crowd of chatter-writers that they were anything but just pals. And, for once, Hollywood believed. Ginger's the sort of regular scout a fellow'd take out just for fun, yet now the gossips are linking her and Howard Hughes.

blackmail cases in Hollywood are reported to my office," the district attorney declares. "Picture people, especially those with big names and big salaries, live in mortal fear of the blackmailer, but when they are victimized they usually 'pay off' rather than take a chance on the publicity."

Mr. Fitts further states that many of Hollywood blackmailers are amateurs, recruited from the ranks of discharged servants, disgruntled poor relations and the "women scorned."

Few stars have had sufficient courage to bring blackmailers into open court. Wally Beery did when he was accused of being the father of an extra girl's illegitimate child. He not only declined to pay hush money—he faced the publicity barrage and proved her claims false. Yet it cost him a small fortune to fight the case. The most dastardly charge can be woven entirely of lies, and yet receive front-page space in every newspaper. No wonder, then, that the star trembles—and pays.

Perhaps, when you noted a bodyguard on the star's payroll, you muttered scornfully, "The big ninny—he must be afraid of the dark."

He is—for during the past two years almost every high-salaried star in Filmtown has received "blackhand" letters, demanding money and threatening everything from kidnaping to murder in the event of a refusal. Gary Cooper, Marlene Dietrich, Mary Pickford, Joan Crawford, Anne Harding, Bebe Daniels, Douglas Fairbanks, Harold Lloyd—they've all been blessed with such friendly little epistles. And how many others have received them, and paid in fearful silence, Allah alone knows!

BEFORE leaving the subject of extortion and blackmail, I again quote Rex Cole:

"At least a dozen times in the past two years, I've been forced to meet blackmail attempts directed against my clients. One of the most common rackets is perfectly illustrated by the most recent attempt.

"A man I know slightly—he's been hanging about the fringe of Hollywood society for years—came into my office and 'warned' me that a 'friend of his' had started a new publication, that this 'publisher' had unearthed a particularly nasty story about a certain client of mine, and that it was in type, ready for printing.

"'The publisher is a mighty good pal of mine,' he urged. 'I think I can persuade him to kill the story, but, of course, he wants to recoup the money he has spent in getting it ready to print. I think he'd listen to reason for—say—$3,000!'

"I told him that we would be delighted to refer the matter to the district attorney. He didn't stop to argue.

"Another petty-larceny form of the same blackmail scheme has been used for years by racketeering publishers who spring up from time to time. They sell high-priced advertising space to the stars by threatening unfavorable criticisms and scandalous stories. Usually, magazines of that sort do not last long."

One of the most contemptible of Hollywood's rackets travels under the

How Much Money?

How Much Money?

guise of charity. Let's give the floor to Conrad Nagel, president of the Motion Picture Relief fund.

"Nine or ten 'fake charity' demands are submitted to the Relief Fund officers every week," he told me. "We estimate that film stars, during the past year, contributed slightly more than $2,000,000 to charity racketeers. This year, because the depression gives such racketeers a better calling card, we will probably contribute even more.

"The fraudulent schemes hiding behind the name of charity are too numerous for detailed exposure. One of the most common is the 'charity ball' given for the 'benefit' of some group of disabled veterans, or, in fact, any other worthy organization. The Legion and the disabled veterans are not to be blamed. They're victimized by the promoter of the ball. He's the man who makes the money.

"The first step in his campaign is to buy a smuggled telephone directory listing the number of every star. When he calls, he is at first unctuous. He urges the star to buy a dozen tickets in order to aid such a deserving cause. If the star refuses, the promoter then begins to use veiled threats. He lists the number of men in the organization which has been persuaded to lend its name to the ball. 'Now, you wouldn't want me to tell all those good theater-goers that you refused to aid them out of your plenty, would you?' Usually the star gives in and buys a few tickets."

A "few tickets" is right! Jack Oakie checked up and found that in thirty days he had paid just $350 for tickets to such "charity" affairs. He's been a tough customer ever since.

Nagel also told me that a recently conducted investigation had revealed that the Relief Fund, itself, was supporting 137 out-and-out "chiselers," men who were not in the slightest need of charity.

IT is impossible to estimate the total amount of money given to professional panhandlers by Hollywood notables, but it must run into many thousands each year. They are as thick as fleas in Hollywood. They cluster in front of each studio, haunt every cafe frequented by the stars and descend like a swarm of locusts on every premiere.

I persuaded a number of them to talk and discovered that Hollywood is known to their craft as "Panhandlers' Paradise." They average "better than wages" and several of them bragged to me that they were taking in as much as sixteen dollars a day! They prefer to "broach" the stars in front of the studios and cafes, for there they can always depend on an audience of star-worshipping sightseers. Before his fans, a star dares not appear stingy.

While investigating Hollywood's panhandlers, I found one who uses glycerine tears to emphasize his sob story, another who fakes a twisted spine, a third who owns an apartment house, and so on, ad infinitum.

Almost every star supports a small army of poor relations. They cannot refuse to do so. What star, publicized as the owner of a $10,000-a-week salary, can afford to have a cousin living in poverty? Mr. and Mrs. Public would hasten to tear down an idol in

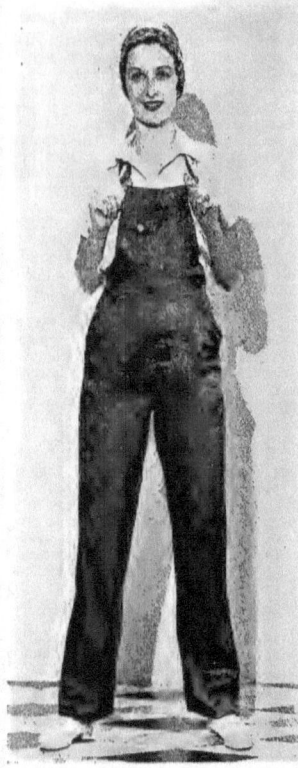

Gail Patrick, wearing her "depression trousers"—bright red cotton overalls, durable, yet gay, and quite inexpensive.

that case. The star knows it, and you can bet your bottom dollar, so does the cousin!

HARKING back to our star's expense sheet, you must have considered certain of the items appallingly high. Perhaps you decided that I am an unmitigated liar. In self-defense, let me submit a few more facts.

For example, there's that item of $225 a week for fan mail expense. Connie Bennett, who does *not* receive more than the average amount of fan mail, spent $12,000 last year on stamps, stationery and professional photographs.

Mary Pickford, at the height of her popularity, received 20,000 fan letters a week.

Francis X. Bushman, at one time, employed *eight* secretaries to answer his mail. Two million copies of one photograph were mailed to his fans.

Tom Mix, last year, spent $13,320 on his fan mail. And, by the way, Tom maintained a staff of thirteen servants, *gave* $22,000 to needy friends, donated $20,000 to organized charity, and spent $7,000 for groceries.

Beach house rentals at Malibu *average* $750 a month, and some run as high as $2,000, which, incidentally, is the amount paid by John Gilbert for his seaside "shack." Beverly Hills mansions of the class demanded by out-

standing stars rent for as much as $3,000 a month.

You pay $75 for a suit and feel extravagant. Players like Wallace Beery, Adolphe Menjou, Douglas Fairbanks, Harold Lloyd and half a hundred others are charged $200 a suit by the exclusive tailors to whom they go. Joan Crawford spends $15,000 a year for clothes, Connie Bennett $12,000.

Much of this money is spent to maintain a reputation. Stars feel that a "rep" for some particular idiosyncrasy is an asset in hand. Mae West's diamonds are part of her publicity campaign. Even Neil Hamilton's jig-saw puzzle fad was responsible for a deluge of press mention. By the way, I remember that he paid $75 for one puzzle in order to support his "reputation."

YOU can take your friends to a medium-priced cafe and still feel that you're an excellent host. Not so the Hollywood star. Because of his position, he is expected to entertain only in the most lavish cafes, order the most expensive food, buy the latest car and sit in the most expensive theater seats. When he travels, he must ride on the best trains, sail on the best ships, fly in the fastest planes and rent the royal hotel suite.

Maybe he's a sap—but ask yourself these questions: "How much of his glamour depends upon his lavish style of living—and how much does his 'box-office appeal,' depend on his glamour?"

At any rate, his follies are his own. At least, they keep money in circulation and benefit society at large.

He could still save money if it were not for lawsuits, fake charities, padded bills, rackets, blackmail and extortion.

I see by today's Los Angeles papers that Colleen Moore is being sued for $100,000 as the result of a minor traffic crash. . . .

It still goes on!

The Real Mae West

Continuing the life story of the Brooklyn Blonde who has shattered every screen tradition

EDITORS NOTE: *So much has been rumored, said and printed about the blonde tornado who has swept aside many of the screen's accepted standards, that NEW MOVIE readers have been asking for the real life story of Mae West. Last month you met her in these pages as the youthful instigator of delightful new mischief for her companions and as she experienced the joys and sorrows of young love. Now go on to her girlhood, her struggles, disappointments and triumphs and why, though men are "crazy" about her, she has not married.*

CANNILY shrewd, totally unaffected, Miss West's witticisms are a mixture of common sense and wisecracks. A young woman wrote to her asking for advice. "What," she asked, "is the best way to hold your man?"

"The best way to hold your man," replied Miss West, "is in your arms."

I asked Miss West one day if she believed to be true what a charming, cosmopolitan elderly lady once remarked to me: "Every woman is a rake at heart."

"Certainly," replied Miss West, "it's all a question of how you direct your energy. I'm sure I could be a very bad woman if I weren't too busy doing other things."

All her life Miss West has devoted herself to the theater, and she knows all phases of it. Burlesque and vaudeville were a natural step forward for the precocious and talented little girl who had graced the stages of the Clarendon Stock Company in Bushwick and Brighton Beach.

"Battling Jack" West, who knew his professional world, wasn't a bit anxious to have his little daughter spend her life among theatrical folks, but Mae's mother, always strongly in sympathy with her, insisted, and the little West child, flaxen curls bobbing up and down in tune with her nimble feet, had studied dancing with Ned Wayburn and was well-rounded, (with her proficiency in child roles behind her) for a varied and promising career. Wayburn remains to this day one of her close and valued friends—characteristically Mae West.

Mae was thirteen years of age when she made her debut in vaudeville, where she was known as the "baby vamp."

At this juncture it might be amusing to hear the story of her first beau. Tired of the knickerbockered lads of her acquaintance, she longed to have a date with a boy who wore long pants. She plotted and schemed,

BY AILEEN ST. JOHN BRENON

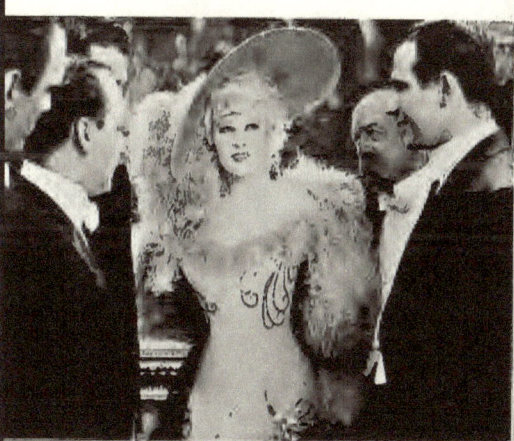

Eugene Robert Richee

Mae West turns on one of the sidelong glances which have aroused so much comment among movie fans. This is a scene from her forthcoming picture "It Ain't No Sin."

Right: A new and heretofore unpublished portrait of the "Queen of the Wisecrackers," reflects the strong individuality and inherent talent which have helped to carry her along the roadway to success.

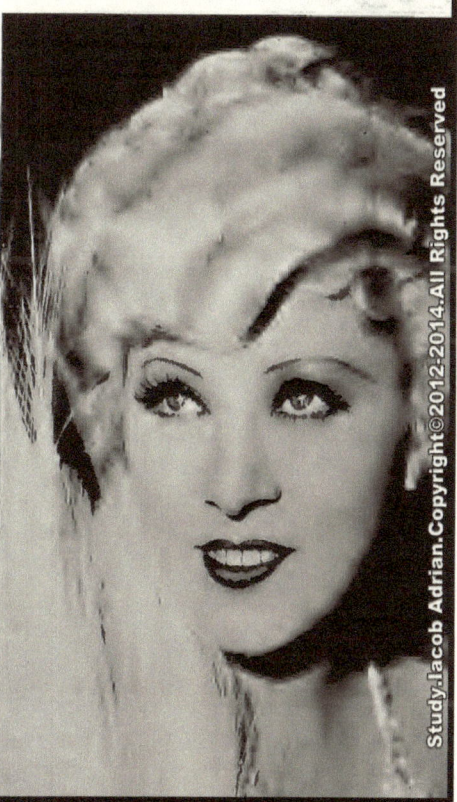

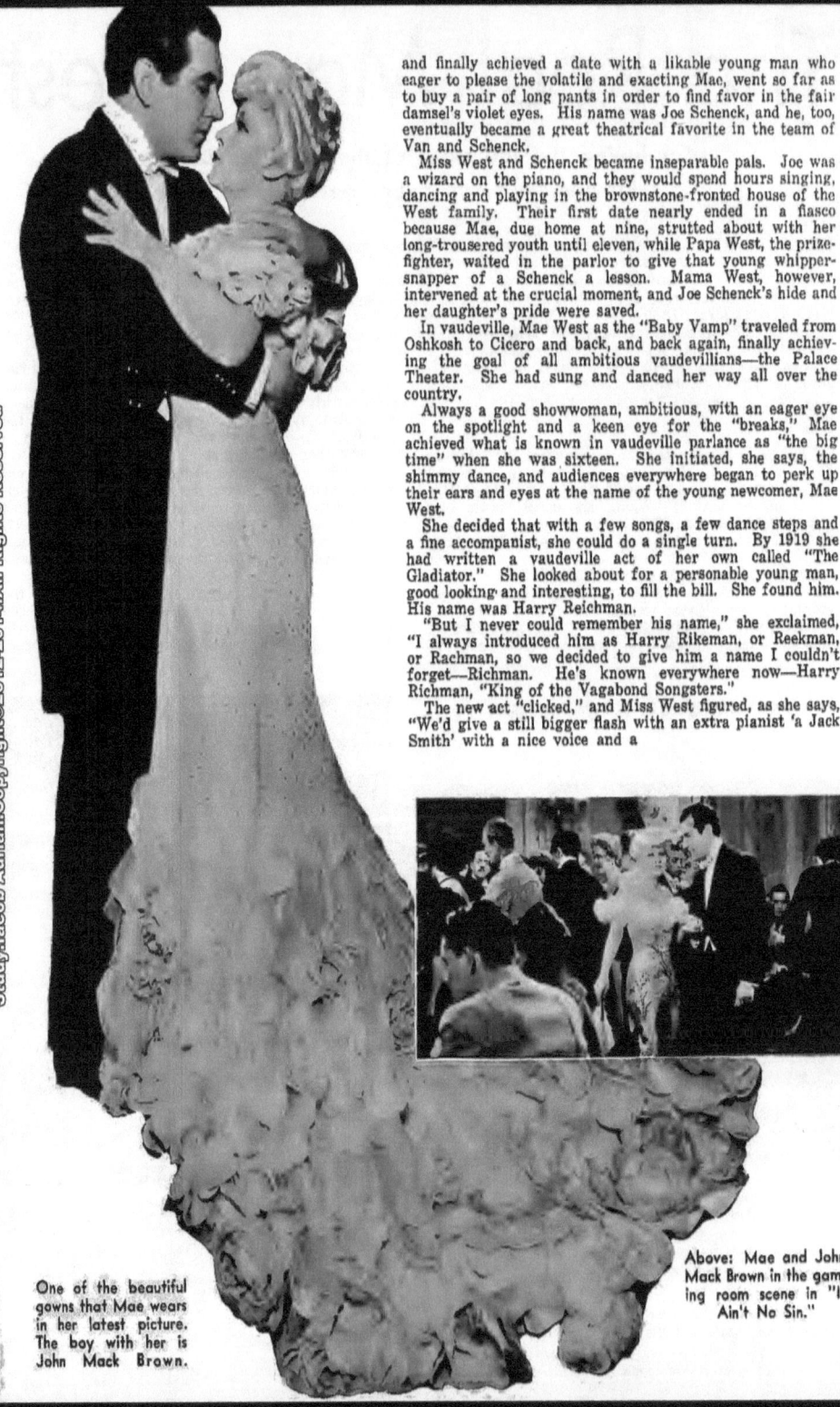

and finally achieved a date with a likable young man who eager to please the volatile and exacting Mae, went so far as to buy a pair of long pants in order to find favor in the fair damsel's violet eyes. His name was Joe Schenck, and he, too, eventually became a great theatrical favorite in the team of Van and Schenck,

Miss West and Schenck became inseparable pals. Joe was a wizard on the piano, and they would spend hours singing, dancing and playing in the brownstone-fronted house of the West family. Their first date nearly ended in a fiasco because Mae, due home at nine, strutted about with her long-trousered youth until eleven, while Papa West, the prize-fighter, waited in the parlor to give that young whipper-snapper of a Schenck a lesson. Mama West, however, intervened at the crucial moment, and Joe Schenck's hide and her daughter's pride were saved.

In vaudeville, Mae West as the "Baby Vamp" traveled from Oshkosh to Cicero and back, and back again, finally achieving the goal of all ambitious vaudevillians—the Palace Theater. She had sung and danced her way all over the country.

Always a good showwoman, ambitious, with an eager eye on the spotlight and a keen eye for the "breaks," Mae achieved what is known in vaudeville parlance as "the big time" when she was sixteen. She initiated, she says, the shimmy dance, and audiences everywhere began to perk up their ears and eyes at the name of the young newcomer, Mae West.

She decided that with a few songs, a few dance steps and a fine accompanist, she could do a single turn. By 1919 she had written a vaudeville act of her own called "The Gladiator." She looked about for a personable young man, good looking and interesting, to fill the bill. She found him. His name was Harry Reichman.

"But I never could remember his name," she exclaimed, "I always introduced him as Harry Rikeman, or Reekman, or Rachman, so we decided to give him a name I couldn't forget—Richman. He's known everywhere now—Harry Richman, "King of the Vagabond Songsters."

The new act "clicked," and Miss West figured, as she says, "We'd give a still bigger flash with an extra pianist 'a Jack Smith' with a nice voice and a

One of the beautiful gowns that Mae wears in her latest picture. The boy with her is John Mack Brown.

Above: Mae and John Mack Brown in the gaming room scene in "It Ain't No Sin."

The Real Mae West

nice personality," and "whispering Jack Smith" was born.

From vaudeville Miss West was booked into a musical show at the old Winter Garden by the Shuberts. Then followed an appearance with Ed Wynn in "Sometime." Later, finding herself back on the road again doing one night stands, she yearned for the brilliance and gayety of the Gay White Way.

In the lexicon of Mae West there is only one way to get what you want—that is, to work for it and take it. She determined to get back to Broadway.

Everything Mae West has, she has worked for—her prominence, her success, her diamonds—the diamonds she loves so well and which are synonymous with Mae West, "Diamond Lil," if you prefer. Nothing has been given to her on a silver platter. She's indignant at the very thought of those who expect something for nothing.

It was while she was on the road that Miss West "got the idea" that she could write a play—with Broadway as the goal.

"I had in mind several stories as possibilities," she said, "and between shows I secluded myself at my hotel or in my dressing room and did some real work."

A play called "Sex" was the result, for which she secured backing and produced herself.

MAE WEST has achieved what she went after—fame, fortune, success, diamonds—but they've come with a stormy and tempestuous career, for after "Sex" had been playing on Broadway a few months, officers of the law stepped in and decreed the performance improper. Court documents and the public prints record the wit and sallies of Mae West at the trial, but judicial opinion prevailing, Miss West, as an enemy of the public good, spent a few days on Welfare Island. She took it with good grace, made friends with the unfortunate girls committed there, and when she left the warden announced, "She's the finest woman I ever met."

It was while playing with Ed Wynn in "Sometime" that she first made the acquaintance of James H. Timony, a successful lawyer, destined to become one of her strongest allies and firmest friends. Anent the possibility of their marriage, Miss West exclaims, "No secret marriage for me. When I marry the whole world is going to know about it!"

Mr. Timony, with his knowledge of show business and politics, and his large acquaintance in New York, has given invaluable advice to Miss West in the management of her business affairs. As actress, writer and producer of plays, she needed a business manager and gradually Timony relinquished his other interests to take complete charge of the management of hers. This business relationship still exists after many years, and those who know Mae West are familiar with the genial, kindly presence of Lawyer Timony, ever present when business is transacted or a legal question needs to be settled.

In explaining why she never married, Miss West, for all her worldly wisdom and hard-boiled wisecracking, is a bit shamefaced at the reason. I may be mistaken, but I'm sure I saw her blush when I asked her. "The truth is, no kidding," she said, "my mother never approved of a single boy friend I had.

"I loved them all—all the boys—and always have had a swell time with them, but whenever I showed up with one who wanted to take me to the altar, my mother didn't like him, and what I saw that, somehow or other I soured on him, too.

"I'm tickled to death I did. I'd probably be married and divorced half a dozen times by now—think of all the trouble that would be.

"I'm telling the boys and girls not to be ashamed to listen to Mama—it saves a lot of alimony and a lot of grief.

"Like men? I've known lots of them, but in later years I've never found one I liked well enough to marry. Besides, marriage is a career in itself and I work too hard at other things. You have to work at marriage, too, to be successful, and until I've time for marriage I'll stay single." And she has.

Mae West is a woman of warm feeling, however. Throughout the years she has remained very close to her family. A brother and a sister followed her footsteps into the theater. The sister, Beverly West, is a widely known vaudeville actress, and the brother, Jack West, Jr., works for one of the well-known film companies in Hollywood.

Nothing has been able to fill the void left by the death of Miss West's mother. Mae lived at home at her mother's house on Long Island, and when Mrs. West died, the daughter never went there again. The house, as the mother left it the day she died, is bolted and barred and deserted. A great deal of Miss West's heart is locked up in that house, for the great love that she had for that kind, wise woman who was her mother, has been one of the biggest things in her life. She went to her for advice, and comfort, and sympathy, and found in the wisdom of the older woman counsel and understanding and help.

Since the death of her mother, Miss West lives with her sister while in New York in the latter's apartment which is on West End Avenue, in the Seventies.

I HAVE seldom seen a day pass in her dressing room at the theater when she was not visited by her father. He is a kindly, genial man, who brings his pals to the theater in those long periods between shows when his hospitable daughter receives the long list of friends she has accumulated in the many years it has taken to climb the ladder of success, as she exclaims, "wrong by wrong."

The friends and acquaintances are always assured—strong and weak alike—of a warm welcome and a wisecrack from the jovial blonde, graceful and alluring in the maroon velvet *peignoir* she wears in her dressing room at the theater.

Miss West invariably has a wad of bills in her stocking for those who may be in need. She is at once shrewd and farseeing, quick to separate the wheat from the chaff. She fights hard any attempt to "put anything over" on her or anyone else. But she never can refuse help where she knows a hard luck tale is true.

She detests crookedness, deceit and insincerity and is unsparing with the "slick artists," but with weak unfortunates of life she is patient and helpful, and many a time I have seen her do little acts of kindness which I will relate later.

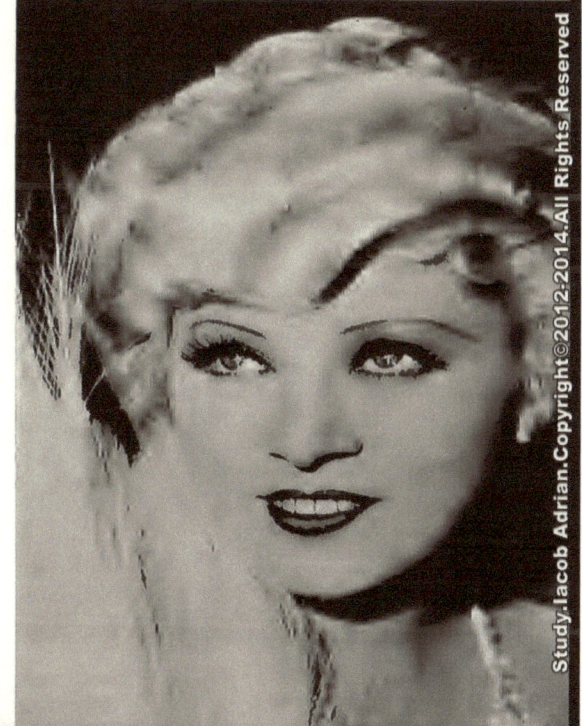

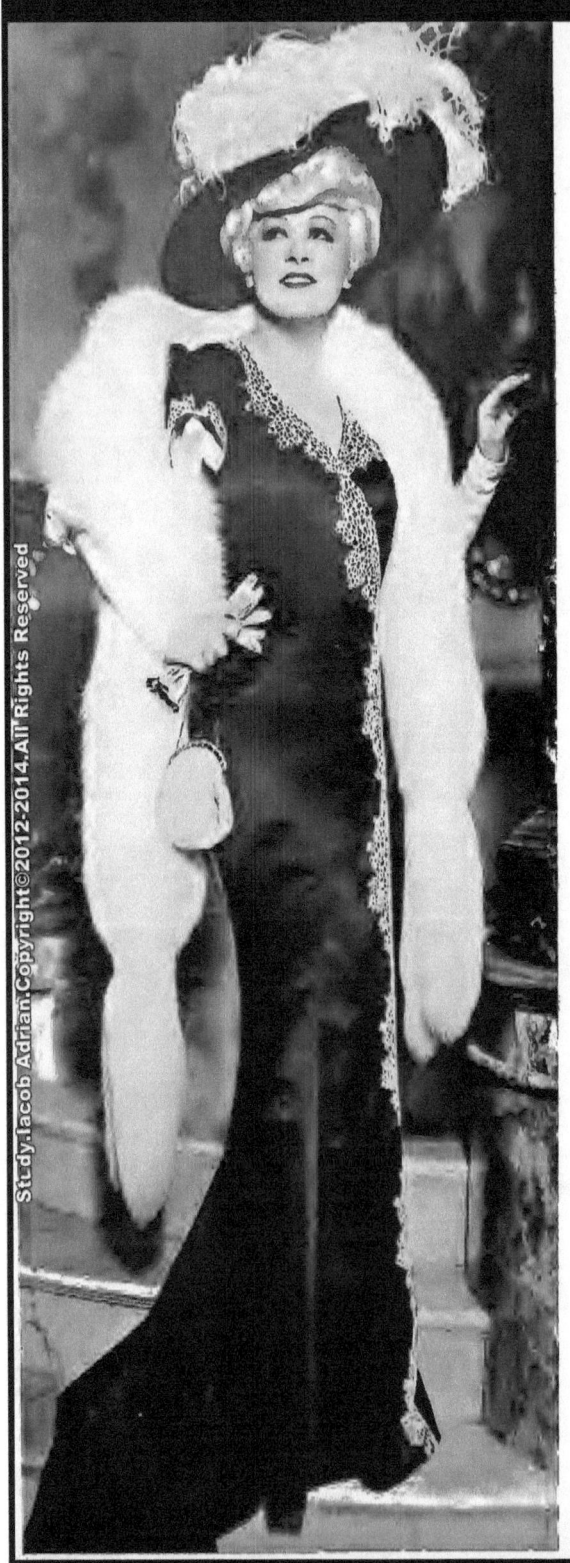

Concluding the life story of the
astonishing Lady of Glamour

The Real
MAE
WEST

By AILEEN ST. JOHN BRENON

POPULAR as Mae West has always been with men—both on and off the stage—Miss West's audiences, strange as it may seem, have been composed for a large part of staid, kindly, middle-aged ladies. You know the sort—solid, shrewd homebodies who have devoted their lives to making their menfolks comfortable throughout the years, humoring their foibles and idiosyncracies, closing their eyes to their faults and shortcomings. These wise ladies, who have more worldly wisdom in their little fingers than their restrained exteriors admit, thoroughly appreciate and enjoy the jokes and sallies of *la* West, at the expense of the *genus homo*.

Mae West explains that the reason people enjoy her rowdy fun is that she makes sex something to laugh about and enjoy, not to cry or wail about, whereas your lachrymose heroine suffers at the expense of, rather than outwits her man.

Women, Mae West believes, have all situations well in hand. She believes with Thackeray that any woman can have any man she wants, provided she hasn't a squint in her eye; but Miss West puts it in her own language, vintage 1934:

"Any woman, no matter how dumb she is, can outsmart any man no matter how brilliant he thinks he is. It's been her job for years. Woman has had to fight her battle throughout the ages with only one weapon—her intuition—and it's become so sharp no man worthy of the name is proof against it.

"This is the greatest age for women. They no longer have to sit primly on a straight-backed chair with hands folded, waiting for some guy to come and make a pass at them.

"She's got her own money, her time's her own, and she goes out and grabs a man for herself—not any man, but the one she wants. If she doesn't like him when she gets him, all she has to do is to go out and take another pick."

Miss West herself prefers ugly men. "The ugly ones," she says, "and the guys with busted noses and cauliflower ears and scrambled pans, especially, you know what I mean—guys with faces not handsome, but strong, like Louis Wolheim. Other women aren't so apt to cast sheep's eyes at them."

In the costume she wears in her latest Paramount picture, "It Ain't No Sin."

With all the slings and arrows she has hurled at convention, Mae West has her own integrities. For example, despite her free

GOOD OR BAD INFLUENCE?

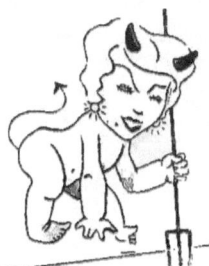

Grandma, Mom, Pop, the Kids—Letters by the hundreds poured in to attack or defend Mae's influence! It seems everybody in the country has his own idea about her. Here are the two prize winners, chosen from hundreds. Do you agree?

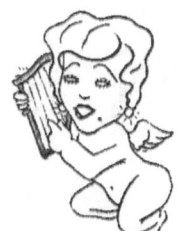

"BAD INFLUENCE"
The letter chosen as best

Mae West is decidedly a bad influence in the movies! Not on the box-office. Not on the older people who attend shows. But on the children of adolescent age who comprise a huge part of movie audiences everywhere. We older ones laugh at her innuendoes, applaud her honesty and come away having thoroughly enjoyed ourselves, where the younger ones take up her attitudes, remarks, and rowdy philosophy of sexy smartness (which the nth degree of sexy smartness as being possibly they are, but that fact makes them no more desirable for adoption by fourteen-year-olds!)

They are unable to enjoy her shows and leave them - the effects reach over into their personal lives, coloring their thoughts and perhaps their actions too decidedly.

Mae West is lauded for her unconventionality, and while we take her pictures with a wink, knowing them for what they are - good entertainment for adults - I think our younger people are prone to take them literally.

MRS. D. WHEATLEY, JR., COMMERCE, TEXAS.

Mae balances public opinion neatly in her two hands.

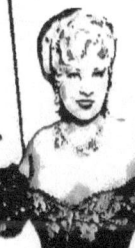

"GOOD INFLUENCE"
The letter chosen as best

Mae West has enriched the screen in many ways. Like an invigorating tonic, she has given a worried world a hearty, rollicking laugh at a time when they needed it most. Not even the most sour-faced, hardened cynic can resist Mae West's clever mannerisms and spontaneous wit and nothing is better for the soul and body than a good, side-splitting, roaring laugh with all the works.

In spite of her vulgar characterizations, she is a good influence because her brazen portrayals hold a revealing mirror up to the young, showing them better than a thousand lectures, how common it looks to be cheap and vulgar.

If Mae West had done nothing else with her buxom, feminine curves, but made scrawny women conscious of their emaciated, unhealthy figures, and put the brakes on this dangerous, dieting craze, she has rendered a great and timely service to the screen and public in general.

And so I say, more power to Mae West. She is an asset to the screen; a gallant pioneer who has blazed a golden trail to exhilarating and unfailing entertainment, which, after all is what the public wants and pays for.

REBA LONDON, ATLANTA, GEORGIA.

Lively letters condemning Mae's influence

Mrs. Joe Miller, Charlotte, N. C.—Children and youth by nature are imitators. Every girl from six to sixteen in my staid Southern village struts a Mae West swagger.

Mrs. Mabel Hewes, Biloxi, Miss.—Someone has written that if a writer, by his writings, cannot make the world one whit better by doing so, he had better lay down his pen. So it is with an actor or actress.

F. J. Bendik, New York City—I consider the salacious Mae West motion pictures the most demoralizing influence of the present day.

Phylis Adato, New Brunswick, N. J.—Mae West could only keep repeating her vulgar roles, which soon enough will disgust

These people have nothing but praise to offer

Mrs. T. E. Carpenter, Jr., Durham, N. C. —If she chooses to commercialize this "certain something" she has, why shouldn't she? Others do!

Mrs. Mary Alice Lallande, Hollywood, Cal.—Born in the early Seventies, I do not recall ever hearing the word "sex" mentioned in conversation. But Time Marches On! Decades progress, grandmothers too.

Jane E. Burtis, Globe, Ariz.—After all the namby-pamby stars who have been dished out, the last few years, she comes as invigorating as a salty sea breeze.

Mrs. R. Skulnick, Brooklyn, N. Y.—Through her hips and curves she has delivered a burning message to the feminine world. It is, in short, "Stay Feminine—First and Always!"

The Real Mae West

and easy ways, her staff addresses her always as "Miss West." She's very particular about that. Those who work for her are her friends always. She gives them loans if they are hard up. She makes their sorrows hers. But they must keep their distance—professionally.

Her response to those suffering from the trials and tribulations of life is as real as it is spontaneous. She has never lost her interest in the plight of the girls she met during her visit to Welfare Island.

In her dressing room one day I asked her if she would recall any kindnesses she has done for women. Her goodness to men out of jobs, to the people of the theater, is proverbial.

"I don't think so much of women," she said. "I can't think of anything I ever did for them—maybe I never have helped any."

As it happened, a young woman and an elderly man were ushered into her dressing room only five minutes later, and Miss West and the two of them went off into secret conclave. To make a long story short, the man was a doctor. The girl had made the acquaintance of Miss West on the Island, and had through unfortunate circumstances taken to relieving her sorrows with dope. Miss West had arranged some days previously to pay hospital expenses for a cure, but was eager to give the doctor the "once over" before putting the girl in his care.

Through long years in the show business, and her experience in dealing with all sorts and conditions of human beings, Miss West has learned to size up people in two minutes, and in her judgment of character she is shrewd, analytical and discerning.

HAVING launched herself on a career of writer, producer and star of her own plays, Miss West's next play was "Pleasure Man," followed by "Diamond Lil," one of the greatest theatrical hits of the past decade. It came to be written in a peculiar way. Coming home one night from the theater, bedecked and shining in her favorite jewels, Miss West was stopped at the desk of her hotel by the manager.

"Excuse me, Miss West," he exclaimed, as brilliant, gay and saucy, she strutted provocatively into the foyer, "but you remind me of an old gal of mine."

"O-ooh?" said Miss West, ever ready to listen to a fellow's yarn.

"Yes," he said, "Diamond Lil, the pride of the Bowery, when I was a lad of parts."

And he launched forth into a description of this notorious gal, easy to get, hard to forget, who claimed men's hearts and wore their diamonds.

Mae West became very curious about this gay and gaudy lady of the romantic nineties who lived in the heart of the elderly hotel manager, as the most glamorous and alluring being he had ever known. He had a trunk full of photographs, gewgaws and mementoes of the unscrupulous, seductive dame who lived and loved on the Bowery.

"Diamond Lil," dead these many years, began to live again in the imagination of Mae West, and day by day the rowdy, restless, roisterous, unregenerate lady with passion unrestrained, became Diamond Lil as we know her on the stage today, blonde, buxom and bejewelled, with wisecracks on her tongue, a promise in her eyes, and no mercy in her heart. Opulent of bosom, waspish of waist, and with those curving hips which have become the fashion, Diamond Lil embarked upon her professional career of luring and outsmarting men a la Mae West.

With the success of "Diamond Lil," Mae West was on the top of the world. Her sallies, "You can be had," and "Come up and see me sometime," were on every tongue, and the clientele of the Mae West show was the most chic and smartest in town. She became the toast of the Gay White Way.

Miss West is five feet four inches tall and weighs 116 pounds. The transformation into the buxom shapeliness required for Diamond Lil exacted of her a strict regime. She had to eat her way to success in order to acquire that superabundance of curves—danger ahead! Diamond Lil—in fact all the beauties of her day—were Junoesque.

With 160 pounds as her goal, she wore a specially constructed boned corset which brought her waist in and her hips out, designed and executed by no less a personage than the maker of Lillian Russell's inimitable armor.

Mae West was playing on the stage when her mother died. Schooled in the tradition of the theater—"the play must go on"—she went ahead with her evening's performance. Hardboiled? When the final curtain went down, a physician had to be sent for to revive her. Overcome by grief and emotion they found Miss West on the floor of her dressing room unconscious.

Miss West loves opulence and richness and gaudiness, in some things. Her clothes are simple but striking, and her jewels, round her throat, at her breast and on her fingers, and up to her arms, are the last word in lavish display. She loves jewels, and one of her real sorrows occurred while in California when she lost one of her most prized possessions. A hold-up man saw fit to relieve her of her favorite pendant—a champagne bottle in diamonds which she wore suspended from a diamond necklace. She was wrathful with that bandit, who forced the door of her limousine in front of her Hollywood apartment. With a pistol at her ribs, she judged this was one of the men who couldn't be had. However, she gave him a piece of her mind, along with the pendant.

Miss West made her debut in Hollywood unostentatiously. Without any heralding or fanfare of trumpets, she went to Hollywood a year and a half ago under contract for a comparatively small part in the picture "Night After Night." She felt that by her performance in that production she would stand or fall in pictures. She asked permission to write her own dialogue, with the result that as the glittering lady whose diamonds were irreconcilable to goodness, she was acclaimed as the hit of the film. And in her next production, "She Done Him Wrong," an adaptation of "Diamond Lil," she was not only catapulted to stardom, but was the reason the picture was the biggest box-office sensation of the year.

In Hollywood she lives simply, in an apartment near the studio, with her brother. She takes part in none of the Hollywood gaieties, spending her time out of the studio writing her dialogue for the current production and preparing the script of the next. Her new one is "It Ain't No Sin." She never misses any of the fights, and Cary Grant, who has accompanied her to some of them, is amazed at the warmth and geniality she brings to the ringside where invariably she greets a host of friends.

"All sorts they are," said Cary Grant on a recent visit to New York. "And she is as interested in them, though she may not have seen them for years, as though she'd been palling around with them the day before. She is interested in human beings, that's the secret of her popularity with them. I don't believe women can appreciate that quality in her.

Miss West's feeling for literature is, like all people whose education has been of their own choosing, spasmodic. But she has a library of biographies of which she is justly proud. It contains the lives of all the great women in history. She hates fiction, because, she says, "I can do my own dreaming; I want to know things that are real."

She likes to portray bad women, she says, because "that's the only kind of women people are interested in. Can you remember any of the good women in history? I can't—only Betsy Ross, and all she could make was a flag!"

Letters Condemning Mae's Influence

practically the whole public.

Robert J. Hill, Dayton, O.—Her talks and lyrics are in many cases an affront and insult to good morals. We are not all perfect morally, but the trend of civilization is for the improvement of morals. Why go backward just to attract those that have not advanced with civilization?

Mrs. John Feehan, Hamden, Conn.— Seeing her picture is much like going to a circus—go once and you know

just what to expect thereafter. Personally I prefer the circus.

Mrs. J. R. Garrison, Knobnoster, Mo.—When one's five-year-old child comes from kindergarten calling, "Yuh kin be had," that's a little more than one can swallow at any time.

Leslie Morton, West Hartlepool, England.—To all conservative people Mae West must appear an unorthodox novelty who is anything but an influence for good.

Letters Condemning Mae's Influence

John Portrum, Columbia, S. C.—Women, in an attempt to imitate her, may resort to the gaudy in both dress and jewelry.

Mae Jones, Philadelphia, Pa.—It is a standard rule in our house that the children, fourteen, seventeen and nineteen, are not to go to any pictures that Mae West appears in. I do so want them to have higher ideals and a little more refinement than they would see paraded before them in any of her pictures. Privately she may be wonderful, but her pictures are just plain vulgar, cheap and disgusting.

These People Have Nothing but Praise

Mrs. Grace Estes, Clarkston, Ga.—Mae West is to the theater-going public what a bright rattle is to a baby, a fairy story and circus to a kid, puppy love to the youngsters.

Betty Virtue Fallin, Medford, Ore.—Who, of the intelligentsia of America, would be morally influenced by a couple of hours at the cinema?

Mrs. R. L. Moreno, Tucson, Ariz.—There are distinctly bad influences in pictures. Among the worst are drunkenness and glorifying gangsters. I have attended every Mae West picture shown in this city, and she hasn't had any such "stuff" as these two things, or been the proverbial "home-wrecker."

Mrs. Ruth Christensen, Catoosa, Okla.—She is a tangy, bitey, phizzy tonic for a depression-ridden people.

Miss Maud O'Bryan, New Orleans, La.—Her antics provide a much needed tonic for over-romanticism and mush, and insidious suggestiveness.

Norman Robertson, Seattle, Wash.—Mae West is a great entertainer. There is a dash of tabasco in her entertainment just s there is a dash of it in her personality. When a personality can make the clothing industry on two continents put on curves, many people are put to work. Incidentally, the wives of two continents get new clothes.

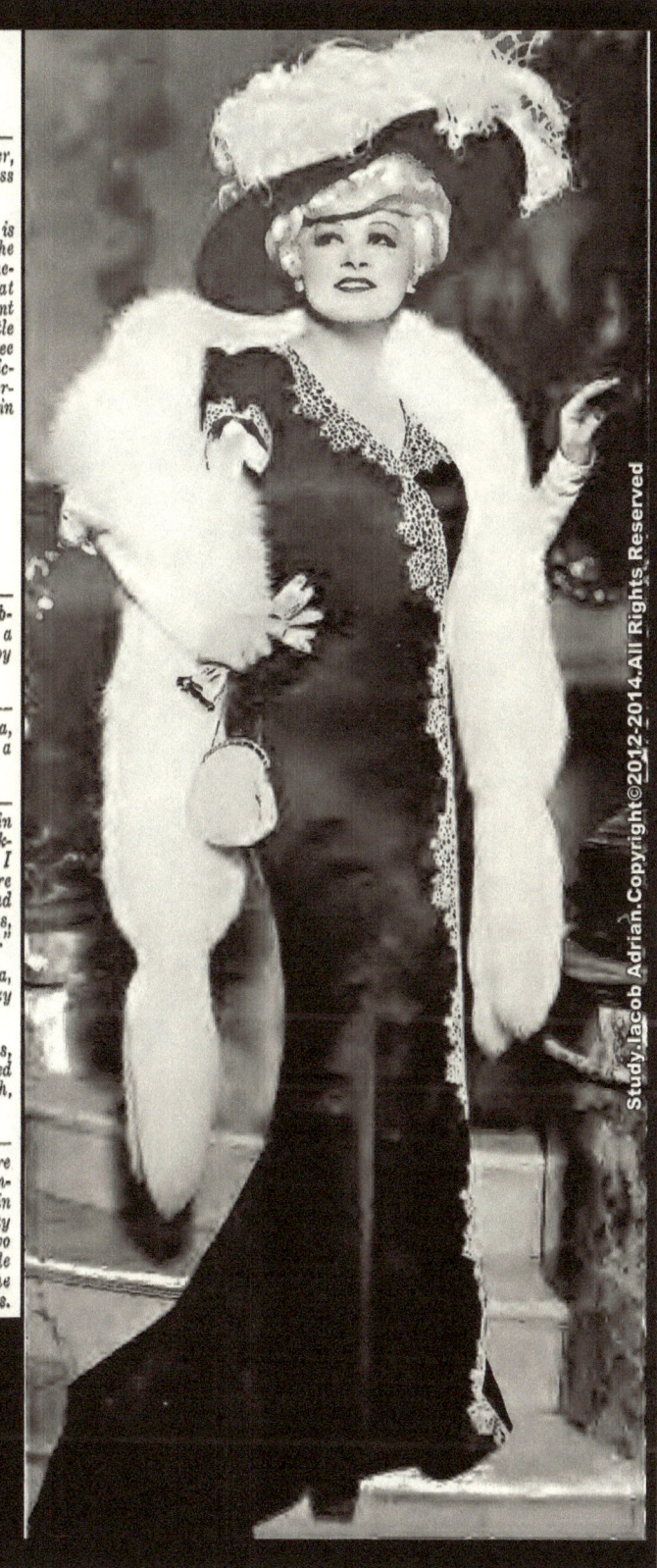

• Coming events cast their shadows before

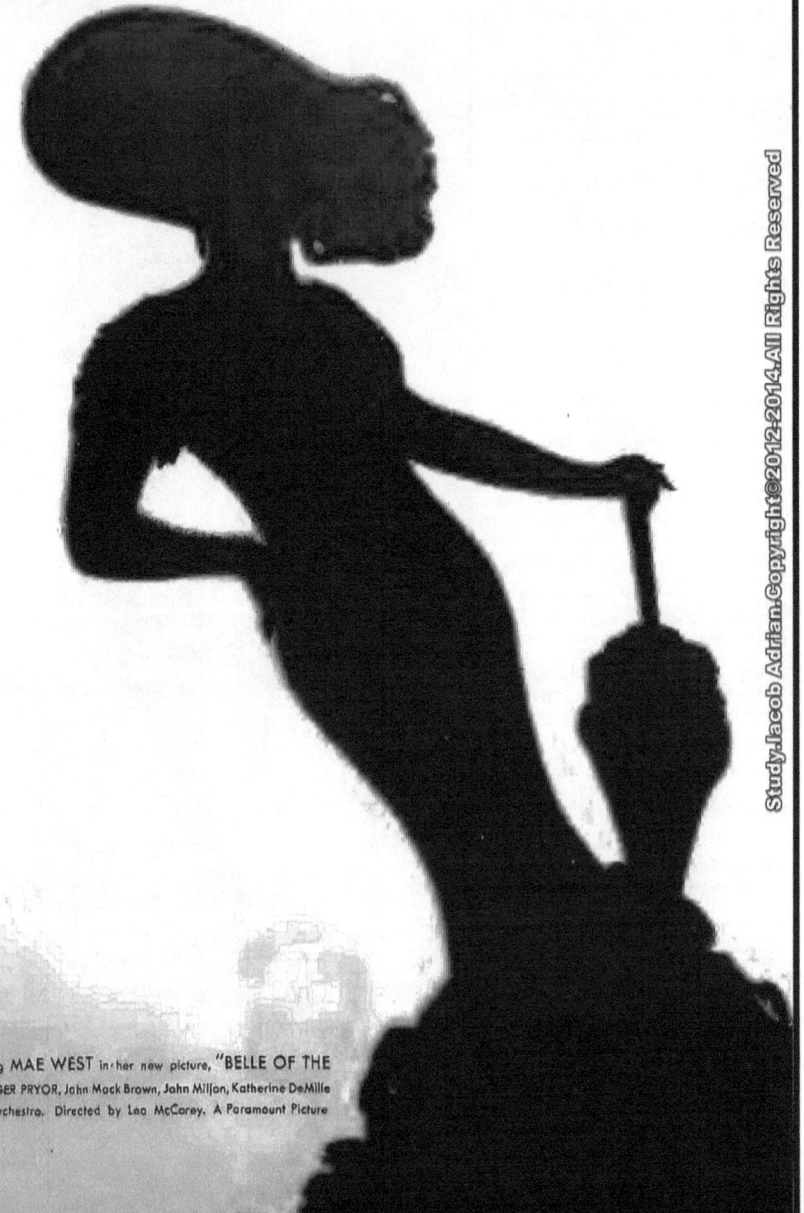

You will soon be seeing MAE WEST in her new picture, "BELLE OF THE NINETIES," with ROGER PRYOR, John Mack Brown, John Miljon, Katherine DeMille and Duke Ellington's Orchestra. Directed by Leo McCarey. A Paramount Picture

Bibliographic sources :

Hollywood (1934-1943)
Publisher: Hollywood Magazine, inc. ; Fawcett Publications, inc.

The New Movie Magazine (1929-1935)
Publisher: Tower Magazines, inc.

This documentary study use,
combined in various proportions,
elements from the following categories,
forms and subsets :
- fair use
- documentary
- documentary photography
- feature
- journalism
- arts journalism
- visual journalism
- photojournalism
- celebrity photography
in order to :
- employ material as the object of cultural critique ,
- quote to illustrate an argument or point ,
- use material in historical sequence,
providing independent opinion,
using photos, press articles, advertisements,
opinions of fans etc. ...